IT'S
ALL
ABOUT
HABITAT

JOSEPH KRUG

Fulton Books, Inc.
Meadville, PA

Published by Fulton Books 2020

Arranged and edited by Jim Krug

ISBN 978-1-64654-729-6 (paperback)
ISBN 978-1-64654-731-9 (hardcover)
ISBN 978-1-64654-730-2 (digital)

Printed in the United States of America

Contents

Part 4: Wider Vision

Part 5: Parting Shots

Foreword

Tribute to a Hero

If Pennsylvania wild turkey hunters were to define a hero, there would be no one more deserving of the title than the late wild turkey biologist Jerry Wunz. The only individual who could challenge Wunz for that title is Roger M. Latham. Latham also was a wild turkey biologist from Pennsylvania and a noted outdoor writer and book author from Pittsburgh.

It was Latham who first concluded that pen-raised wild turkeys could not possibly replicate the superior genetics of wild turkeys that survived nature's culling process in the wild. It is estimated that less than 3 percent of pen-raised turkeys survived more than several months after being released into the wild. Game-farm birds were expensive to propagate, and they proved to be little more than gun fodder for hunters.

Unfortunately, before Latham had the opportunity to press for the discontinued use of game-farm turkeys, he succumbed to a fatal heart attack while vacationing in Sweden. Latham's untimely death fostered a need for someone to take over where he had left off.

Jerry Wunz, the Pennsylvania Game Commission biologist, was convinced of the wisdom of Latham's conclusions and decided to see the game-farm turkey issue put to rest. Wunz realized that a difficult road lay ahead of him if he was to resolve this sensitive political issue. Sportsmen demanded game-farm turkeys. Politicians applied pressure in order to pacify disgruntled hunters and preserve jobs at the game farm. Livelihoods and careers were at stake, and people in high places were committed to game farms.

Wunz, a man of high moral conviction, determined to persevere. He dug in his heels and prepared for a struggle. Unfortunately for Jerry, sometimes management does not appreciate workers who are not submissive. He was called to Harrisburg headquarters and sternly rebuked by his superiors, and temporarily suspended of his duties. When word of Wunz's suspension reached the Pennsylvania Wild Turkey Federation, outraged members went ballistic! Fortunately, this was a fast-growing organization that was rapidly developing its own political muscle. The angry members lobbied behind Jerry and his cause. The political fallout spilled over into the state of Maryland, which requested that if the Pennsylvania Game Commission were to continue to stock pen-raised birds, the Maryland Department of Wildlife did not want any turkeys released closer than 25 miles from its border.

With the political winds shifting, the upper management level of the game commission was taking heat from all directions. Wunz was called back to Harrisburg and reinstated as a wildlife biologist. In the following months, much discussion went into resolving the turkey game-farm issue. Ultimately, the turkey propagation farm was ordered to cease operations, and all breeding stock in the facilities possession would be dispersed.

With pen-raised turkeys now a thing of the past, it was time to take turkey management in a new direction. Any future release of turkeys would utilize birds trapped from the wild by means of cannon or rocket nets. These wild birds were immediately successful in establishing wild turkey populations in regions where repeated stockings of pen-raised turkeys had failed. New breeding flocks were rapidly established as fast as wild birds could be acquired and transplanted. The birds from this trap and transfer program quickly adapted and prospered in areas that were formerly considered unsuitable for turkeys.

Due to the wisdom, courage, and determination of a resolute wildlife biologist, wild turkeys can now be found in every county in Pennsylvania. The stories of Pennsylvania's success in wild turkey management spilled quickly into other states, which soon followed Pennsylvania's lead. As a result of the trap and transplant of wild turkeys, these magnificent birds now occupy almost all suitable habitat in North America. It was not until the immediate success of utilizing wild turkey stock sank in that wildlife managers realized how ineffective the game-farm turkey propagation program had been.

Jerry Wunz passed away on February 4, 2004. He had become a close personal friend, and I miss him dearly. Jerry was a constant source of encouragement and guidance for me. Even though he had a master's degree in wildlife management, he was not the least bit concerned that his newfound friend had zero formal education in the same field. His words, "Joe, you need to write a book," have been kicking around in my head far too long.

Writing this manual is in no way an effort to benefit financially. I have witnessed too many situations where good people expend much energy, money, and resources and receive almost nothing in return for their efforts in habitat work. Both you and our wildlife resources deserve better!

I am confident that if you follow the information in this manual, your efforts will be greatly rewarded. That alone will be enough reward for any efforts of mine, and I know the results will bring a huge smile to my friend Jerry Wunz's face as well.

May all your efforts bear fruit.

Joe Krug
Portage, Pennsylvania

About the Contents

Choosing the title of this book was, by far, one of the easiest decisions made in my efforts to compile a quality habitat-enhancement guideline manual. It is truly all about habitat. If we are to sustain stable wildlife populations, we must have quality wildlife habitat. Refraining from harvesting female deer or hen turkeys in an effort to increase their numbers beyond the carrying capacity of our forests is a recipe for disaster. Unfortunately, this is a fact that many sportsmen are reluctant to accept.

Sometimes, the best wildlife habitat improvement tool we have (when used legally) is the gun. If you are hesitant to embrace this fact, I suggest you enjoy the short-term gratification of artificially high deer populations because the *long-term consequences* are certain to follow. Trust me—you won't like the repercussions, and neither will your children and grandchildren.

I encourage all sportsmen to support and embrace the recommendations of our professional biologists and foresters who are entrusted with the care and protection of our wildlife resources. These are the people who have the training and expertise necessary to make the delicate decisions that best serve the resource and the hunter.

Fortunately, there are many methods for improving habitat and increasing the ability of our forests to sustain wildlife. Almost any tree, shrub, bush, or vine that produces fruit, nuts, or seeds will benefit wildlife. Unfortunately, it is neither possible nor practical for me to attempt to cover all these options. So I will limit my educational efforts to a number of species that will give the reader promising results.

I will cover the positives and negatives of each tree and shrub species that I recommend. Also discussed will be methods of establishing herbaceous openings (HBOs) for wild turkeys and deer. Managing HBOs for deer can require a slightly different approach than those managed for turkeys. I have no formal education in wildlife management. The majority of my training was earned in the proverbial "School of Hard Knocks." If you closely follow the instructions in the manual, you won't have to go there!

For more than thirty-five years of growing, planting, caring, and experimenting with just about anything that grows was a better education than anything I would have received in a classroom. At times, there is no substitute for hands-on experience. Coupled with the tutelage by one of the best wildlife biologists in the business has given me the confidence and experience necessary to provide you with some helpful and useful information. The majority of these instructional efforts are directed toward establishing fruit-producing trees. Fortunately, these same techniques will work equally well in establishing trees that produce hard mast.

Why Do I Plant Fruit Trees?

Species such as apple, pear, and crab apple consistently produce large volumes of fruit for wildlife. For example, a mature apple tree can easily produce ten to fifteen bushels of carbohydrate-rich fruit. This abundance of food can greatly reduce the pressure and stress that foraging whitetails can inflict on a forest. A deer with a belly full of fruit will consume far fewer tree seedlings than a deer with an empty stomach. It's not rocket science.

How to Be Confident That Your Tree-Planting Efforts Will Be Successful

My first attempt at planting a fruit tree proved to be little more than lesson one in the school of hard knocks! I dug an undersized hole, stuffed and forced the tree's roots into it, and tamped some dirt around the crowded root system. The young fruit tree struggled to cling to life for a couple of years before succumbing to the elements. Eventually, I replaced the dead tree with new stock and utilized a better approach for my planting technique.

Lessons learned:

A. For a price, planting stock can be replaced, but time can never be replaced.
B. If you don't do things properly the first time, you will replicate your efforts.
C. Replacement stock is available, but at a cost.

The Ten Commandments were carved in stone to give us guidelines for a happy, productive life. My ten commandments for planting fruit trees are designed to help you be successful and happy with the results.

PART 1

The Basics

Ten Commandments of Planting Fruit Trees

1. Choose a location where the tree will have adequate sunlight and space to grow and flourish.
2. Prepare a washtub-sized hole in which to plant the bare root tree.
3. Select only standard-sized fruit tree-planting tree stock. Avoid, avoid, avoid using dwarf or semi-dwarf stock.
4. Select fruit cultivars that are disease-resistant.
5. Space the young trees at adequate distances.
6. Make absolutely certain to provide the tree with a good trunk protector.
7. Don't even consider planting a tree without providing it with a protective wire cage.
8. Maintain a vegetation-free zone around the young tree.
9. Have a plan in place to deal with trunk borers.
10. Give the trees an occasional application of fertilizer and lime.

In an effort to help you understand the importance of these guidelines, I will discuss each commandment on an individual basis.

Commandment I

Sunlight and space are of utmost importance if the tree is to grow and prosper. Choosing a good location is probably the most important step in planting any tree but especially so with a fruit tree.

Almost on a yearly basis, I find that well-intentioned people have planted fruit trees directly beneath an overhead forest canopy. These plantings have zero chance of surviving! Yes, you may occasionally find old apple trees growing in the forest but must recognize when these trees established themselves. The area was most likely being utilized for agricultural crops or pastureland when those trees were planted.

Pear tree on left was planted twenty-five feet from the edge of woods and had one foot of growth after three years. Pear tree beside it—planted on the same day—was fifty feet from the forest and exhibited thirteen feet of growth!

If your food plots are small, it is advisable to plant your trees near the center of your HBO. On larger plots, trees should be planted at least fifty feet from the forest edge. Remember, you want to keep all trees well away from the root zone of the surrounding hardwoods. Tree roots will extend well beyond the dripline of their branches. Too close and the encroaching trees will rob water, sunlight, and nutrients from the young trees.

Apple tree on the left was planted twenty-five feet from the forest edge. Apple tree beside it—again, planted on the same day—was sixty feet from the tree edge and demonstrated superior growth.

Trees planted too close to the woods have a tendency to grow away from the surrounding forest and toward the sunlight, developing trees that lean. When small, this is of little concern. However, when the tree approaches peak bearing years, it is a condition that is usually fatal to the tree.

Trees that lean off-center are prone to topple when subjected to heavy out-of-balance fruit loads. Remember, you want fruit, not firewood.

Commandment II

Prepare a washtub-sized hole to plant the bare rootstock. I usually scatter about a one-fourth cup of 10–10–10 fertilizer on the bottom of the hole before I plant the tree. If topsoil is available, fill the entire hole with it. If you are short on topsoil, utilize it on the bottom of the hole and around the root zone. Clay and subsoil can be used to fill the rest of the hole.

I grow my own fruit trees in five-gallon buckets, which serve as pots. With container-grown trees, transplant shock is minimized, and a much-smaller hole is satisfactory. It is a huge advantage to plant potted trees. They are more expensive, but their survival rate is much higher, and labor requirements are greatly reduced.

Commandment III

Select nursery stock, which produces standard-sized trees. Avoid all dwarf or semi-dwarf-tree stock. It is true that some semidwarf trees, under highly professional care, will outproduce standards. To achieve these results, however, requires a much higher number of trees per acre, under more intensive management. Semidwarfs require more care and are terribly labor-intensive.

Semidwarf fruit trees being wind thrown due to weak root systems—a condition that will worsen as the tree continues to grow

Dwarf and semidwarf trees are propagated by grafting desirable species of apples onto a nonaggressive rootstock. Unfortunately, nonaggressive rootstocks produce trees that are not well anchored and topple easily. In commercial orchards, all dwarfing trees are usually trellised with wire or staked with support.

I have witnessed semidwarf apple trees up to 8 inches in trunk diameter that black bears have toppled. I have never seen a standard-sized apple tree toppled by a bear.

Standard-sized rootstock is produced by grafting suitable species of apples onto rootstock that has been grown from apple seeds. Semidwarf stock utilizes root sprouts from cloned, non-aggressive root systems.

A tree's graft is usually six to twelve inches above the soil line. Look closely for a change in the color of the bark or a slight crook in the trunk of the young tree. Plant the tree deeper than the graft union, and it will develop into a well-anchored standard-sized tree. If you cannot find standard non-rooted trees, your best option is to plant your semidwarf's graft union (the point where the tree was grafted) below the soil line.

Commandment IV

Select fruit cultivars that are disease resistant. The majority of our most popular species of apples and pears have a low resistance to diseases such as apple scab and fire blight. In commercial orchards, these diseases are controlled by adding fungicides to the pesticide mix, and the trees are sprayed about every six to ten days.

In the wild, regular spray programs are almost impossible to maintain. Your only practical option is to plant fruit (cultivars) varieties that are disease resistant. Thumb through the pages of fruit nursery mail-order catalogs because they are constantly introducing disease-resistant cultivars.

To better understand how fruit tree diseases and fungi negatively impact trees, be certain to read "Apple Choices" and "Pear Choices" in this manual.

Commandment V

Space the trees at proper distances. Tree spacing is far more important than most people realize. Plant trees too close together, and they will attempt to grow away from each other in an effort to maximize crown size. Trees that grow away from their counterparts tend to become "leaners." When the trees are small, it is of little concern. When they become larger, they develop into "leaners" and eventually topple because of an out-of-balance, off-center fruit load. Nothing is more depressing than losing a large healthy fruit tree just as it is reaching peak production capacity. Spacing is so very vital!

Apple trees should be spaced thirty-five feet apart. Pear trees tend to produce a more vertical growth, and a twenty-five-foot spacing is acceptable. A twenty-five-foot spacing is satisfactory for crab apple. Hawthorn trees can be spaced much closer—fifteen feet is acceptable.

Commandment VI

> *A PVC trunk protector was expanding to accommodate a fast-growing fruit tree. The trunk guard could be removed at this time if the grass cover is eliminated.*

Provide young trees with a good trunk protector. Don't even think of planting trees without a trunk protector. Choose to ignore this advice, and you will quickly become an observer as to how quickly mice, voles, and rabbits can devastate the newly planted nursery stock. It might take these rodents two, three, or four years to find these trees, but when they do (and they will), the results are always the same—complete destruction. Remember, you can replace the trees (expensive and labor-intensive), but time can never be replaced.

For a complete understanding of how to deal with rodents, read "Tree Protection Systems" in this manual.

Commandment VII

> *Metal rebar post weaved through and around horizontal and vertical wire mesh eliminates the need for twist ties and allows for cage adjustments.*

Use a protective wire cage to safeguard the young tree. A wire cage will protect the trees from browsing whitetails and rut-crazed bucks who like to rub their antlers on the thick, soft bark of young fruit trees.

If you utilize field fencing (sometimes referred to as cattle wire), make sure to keep the tighter weave of the wire on the *top* part of your cage. If you place the more open weave at the top of the cage, deer can and will poke their heads through the cage and browse the top of the trees. They will do this repeatedly, and eventually, it will kill the trees.

Also, make sure to keep the cage suspended one foot above the ground. This is extremely important! Keeping the cage elevated will allow fox and coyotes to assist you in your rodent management program. Set the cage on the ground, and you have created a safe house for undesirable, destructive creatures. Worse, yet, deer can now reach directly over the cage and browse the crown of the young tree bare.

For a better understanding of how to protect your trees, please read carefully and intently "Tree Protection Systems" in the manual. Also note—if you are planting where elk are present, you are going to have to double the size of your cage and use four metal posts instead of two.

If possible, avoid using wooden stakes. The frost will heave them, and they will need reset yearly, which is a lot of work. When fashioning your wire cages, eight lineal feet of wire is needed to make a suitable-sized cage. If you are dealing with elk, double that to sixteen lineal feet.

Commandment VIII

Maintain a vegetation-free zone around the tree. Don't underestimate the importance of this step! Vegetation and grasses not only rob young trees of water and nutrients, but they also provide mice and voles the cover they need to do their dirty work. Eliminate cover, and you eliminate problems that attract these pests.

The vegetation-free zone should extend outward three to four feet from the tree trunk. This ground cover control program should remain in place until the tree reaches a trunk diameter of five to six inches—longer if you choose to err on the side of safety. By controlling the vegetation around the tree, you will witness close to double the rate of tree growth.

Remember that the faster the tree grows, the sooner it is no longer vulnerable to insects, disease, drought, deer and bear damage that can destroy it.

When applying herbicide with a sprayer, *do not* use the same sprayer to apply insecticides to any part of your fruit trees. You cannot rinse or clean your spray applicator enough to remove all the traces of herbicide. I paint the spray wands of my herbicide bright red to avoid any potential mix-ups.

While many herbicides can be beneficial if properly applied, roundup is my recommendation for those new to habitat management as it is the only herbicide recommended by the Pennsylvania Game Commission. But understand, there is no room for error. Still, I have seen a young tree die when only a cluster of leaves were accidentally exposed to herbicide by a careless sprayer! In the event of an errant spray, stop and snip off all affected leaves before continuing.

Commandment IX

Have a plan to deal with trunk-boring insects. Trunk borers are a very serious problem for young fruit trees. If you lack knowledge on how to deal with the larvae of this insect, be prepared to deal with very high tree losses. There are numerous species of borers in this family—some native, some alien introductions. Borer larvae do their damage by burrowing into the tree's bark and feasting on the nutrient-transmitting cambium layer. If the young grubs encircle the tree trunk one time, it will kill the tree.

Regardless of what type of environment in which you plant the trees, you should constantly monitor them for the presence of this destructive pest. If your plantings are located even remotely close to timber cuttings or anyplace where sapling regenerations are happening, trunk borers are already present, and they will find your trees too.

For a complete understanding of how to deal with his pest, please refer to "Dealing with Trunk Borers" in this manual.

Commandment X

Give your trees an occasional application of fertilizer.

"Joe, my apple tree never gets any apples on it. What is the problem?" is a question I am constantly asked. I usually answer with a question, "Do you ever give it any fertilizer?" I usually get the same response: "You don't have to fertilize apple trees, do you?" My rejoinder is always "No, not unless you want them bear fruit."

Unfertilized trees will produce fruit periodically. Fertilized trees produce on an almost-yearly basis. Not only will they produce fruit more consistently, but they will also produce heavier yields, and the trees will be healthier. Mortality from trunk borers will be significantly reduced.

Crab apple one year after receiving an application of fertilizer

How much fertilizer should you provide for a tree? A good rule of thumb is about one pound of 10–10–10 to an inch of trunk diameter. For example, a five-inch trunk diameter tree will require five pounds of fertilizer, and a ten-inch diameter tree would require ten pounds of fertilizer.

How often should you fertilize? I recommend fertilizing almost yearly. About every third year, I skip the nutrient application. A nutrient buildup can cause your trees to lodge and stop growing. Better too little fertilizer than too much. You can get too much of a good thing.

Mid-March is the best time to apply fertilizer. Summertime applications should be made prior to a forecast of precipitation. If the nitrogen within the fertilizer is not watered into the soil, it will rapidly sublimate the solid pellets transitioning directly to gas and will be consumed in the atmosphere.

Seven Deadly Sins of Fruit Tree Planting

1. Failing to provide a tree with a quality trunk protector
    Without proper trunk protection, the survival of young trees is doubtful at best.

2. Failing to control competing vegetation around young trees
    Dense vegetation competes with the tree for water and nutrients and provides cover and food for mice and voles (bad neighbors).

3. Protective wire cages around young trees (sitting on the ground) not tall enough to protect the top of the tree from foraging deer
    Browse damage suppresses a young tree by inhibiting growth and keeping the tree small and vulnerable to a Pandora's box of problems.

4. Removing protective wire cages and trunk protectors too soon
    Yes, the upper branches of the young tree may be out of reach of deer, but the thick, soft bark on the trunk will not escape the notice of a buck in rut. It's a good tree for a buck to rub his antlers on but very bad for the health of the tree. Remember, you can remove the cage too soon, but you cannot leave it on too long.

5. Failure to anticipate the growth of trees and the surrounding forest

    Consequences can include not adequate room for the tree to reach full maturity size which causes the tree to develop into a leaner by growing toward unrestricted sunlight and allows any shrubs to be overtaken and choked out by faster or larger growing tree species.

6. Not augmenting young trees with proper amounts of lime and fertilizer

    If you are working with acidic soils, and most are, an occasional application of lime is helpful. Consequences of nutrient deficiencies range from stunted trees, slow or low-fruit production, and increased attacks from trunk borers. A tree that stays too small for too long rarely survives.

7. Allowing young apple trees to develop double centers

    A double-centered tree is structurally weak and cannot support a heavy load of fruit. Just about the time your tree is reaching peak-fruit production, a heavy fruit load will cause it to split at the union of the double trunk, reducing its usefulness to firewood.

I refer to these seven things as "deadly sins" of fruit tree establishment because they are exactly that deadly to the survival of the tree. If you want your trees to thrive and prosper, you are usually looking at a six- to ten-year commitment with some routine maintenance on a yearly basis.

May all your efforts bear fruit!

PART 2

Species

Profiles in Habitat

As you can see, planting fruit trees requires developing a plan and follow-up care as well. If you are not willing to provide care for your young trees for their first six to ten years, prepare to be disappointed. I have tried all the shortcuts. Trust me, they don't work!

Before you become discouraged by the efforts required, consider this—a good fruit tree can produce huge volumes of fruit on a near-yearly basis for the next fifty to one hundred years. You will have some effort in caring for young trees, but when they start to produce fruit, the results will awaken in your great energy and enthusiasm. And don't forget—a fruit tree can be a real honey hole for the hunter and can provide a lifetime of enjoyment and satisfaction.

Now that we have discussed how to plant, it is time to consider what to plant. The species that we are going to highlight are trees and shrubs that will give you good results.

Domestic Apples and Crab Apples

If you choose to plant domestic apples, it is important that you plant cultivars that are disease resistant. Unfortunately, the majority of cultivars available in your local lawn and garden shop are very susceptible to fungi and disease. If you want disease-resistance varieties, you probably are going to revert to the mail-order nurseries. Gurneys, South Meadows, Morse, and Stark Brothers all carry disease-resistant varieties. Their catalogs will list these disease-resistant strains.

To better understand the importance of planting disease-resistant strains, please read "Apple Choices" in the instruction manual.

Crab Apples

Crab apple trees tend to be more disease-resistant than apples. Cultivars, such as Indian Magic, Sargent, and Asiatic Crabs, will hold their fruit throughout the winter months and are a better choice for wild turkeys. Species that purge their fruit early, such as Dolgo and Wixon, are probably better suited to deer management. Even in my backyard orchard, I have a strong preference for the disease-resistant varieties.

A very healthy young Dolgo crab

Asiatic crabs distributed by the Pennsylvania Game Commission are very productive and extremely hardy. These seedlings are nongrafted; therefore, their fruit size and color are not predictable. The color of the fruit on these trees will range from red to orange to yellow. Fruit size ranges from pea to quarter-sized.

Asiatic crabs are extremely adaptive and will grow vigorously on the poorest strip mine soils, and they tolerate poorly drained locations quite well. However, they are moderately vulnerable to trunk borers.

Apple trees usually don't fare well in poorly drained conditions, and an Asiatic crab apple or Washington hawthorn would perform better here.

Domestic Pear

The majority of my fruit tree-planting experience is with apples and crab apples. In recent years, however, I have shifted more of my effort to pears with striking results. I am especially impressed with their ability to thrive on the very poorest soil types, even those rocky clay soils on reclaimed strip mines. This hardy pioneer species seldom even needs fertilizer applications to take hold in such otherwise hostile environs.

Pears also grow much faster than apples, and they have very disease-resistant foliage. Unfortunately, many varieties are highly susceptible to fire blight—a deadly tree disease. To better understand fire blight and how to control it, please read "Pear Choices" in this manual.

Note that I put much emphasis on reclaimed surface mine sites. The potential to improve or enhance wildlife habitat on these locations is nearly unlimited.

Washington Hawthorn

Having more than forty years of experience in enhancing wildlife habitat has enabled me to observe the growth and survivability characteristics of numerous species of trees and shrubs. Domestic apple, for instance, will require considerable attention for at least five or ten years in order to have a reasonable shot at survival. Species such as hawthorn and crab apple are far less labor-intensive and easier to establish and maintain.

Washington hawthorn growing on sterile strip mine soil with a good fruit load

There is a fairly long list of trees, shrubs, and vines that can successfully be used to improve wildlife habitat. All have their strong and weak points. If I were forced to pick just one species to work with for wild turkey management, however, it would be Washington hawthorn. Hawthorn is one tough and durable little tree. It thrives in soil types that range from heavy and wet to dry and acidic. I have observed hawthorn exhibiting reasonable vigor on the sterile soil of a reclaimed strip mine. Hawthorn also has good resistance to chewing insects. With the exception of severe insect manifestations, it seldom requires pesticide application.

Adaptable, dependable, hardy, tough, and productive are words I use to describe this species. They are nearly identical to our native species of hawthorns in every capacity but fruit size. Washington hawthorn has clusters of small pea-sized fruit that hang on the branches until the new buds push them off the following spring. This is a species that proves especially beneficial to wild turkeys, grouse, and songbirds.

Trunk borers, which can wreak havoc on apple trees, rarely ever kill hawthorn. If insect control ever becomes an issue with hawthorn, the only insecticide I recommend is Liquid Seven. Most other pesticides will scorch the leaves severely, and several applications will probably kill the tree.

Black bears can be quite destructive to hawthorns despite the tree's being pricklier than a pincushion. It's unbelievable! Don't ask me to explain how bears climb them. It hardly seems possible.

Like most trees, hawthorn prefers total sunlight for maximum vigor. It will tolerate a reasonable amount of shade and, at times, be found growing as an understory species.

Washington hawthorn blooms very late—late June to early July—thereby avoiding frost damage to its blossoms. I cannot ever remember a year when hawthorns did not produce fruit. All these wonderful characteristics have made Washington hawthorn a real favorite of professional landscapers. It has been heavily used in plantings around government buildings, office complexes, and interstate highway interchanges.

Washington hawthorn is not native to Pennsylvania, but its natural range extends into the northernmost parts of Virginia, making it a next-door neighbor. Growth characteristics of the Washington hawthorn are almost indistinguishable from our native Pennsylvania species of hawthorn. A quick glance at the fruit, however, will render it quickly identifiable.

Native hawthorn produces dime-sized fruits that are purged from the tree in early October. The fruits of Washington hawthorn are only pea-sized but hang in large clusters. In contrast to the native hawthorn, Washington hawthorn berries cling to the twigs until the following spring before the tree purges them. This special quality makes an excellent choice as a winter-survival food source for wild turkeys. Although turkeys consume the fruits of our native hawthorn, it is a tree that is perhaps better suited for deer management because the native trees purge their fruits through October.

Do you want to do something positive for wildlife? Plant a couple of hawthorn trees around your hunting camp or on the "back forty." The display of brilliant red fruit on a winter day will warm your heart and please the eye.

As always, provide your new tree with a good trunk protector to ward off mice and rabbit issues. A good wire cylinder fashioned from eight linear feet of cattle fencing will keep the deer away. Do not be naive and think you can avoid either of these steps. Thirty-five years of experience has taught me this—do it right the first time, or you will do it again.

Sawtooth Oak

Young sawtooth oak (L) and Chinese chestnut (R) are growing on surface mine soils, abundant with blossoms. Chestnut is usually heavily suppressed by the foraging deer.

It was late September, and I managed to find some time to do some preseason scouting for the upcoming archery season. Always preferring to kill two birds with one stone, I would also look in on some sawtooth oak plantings.

As I approached the young trees, my optimism escalated. From a distance, I could tell that the trees were considerably larger than during my last visit. Hopefully, they would now be producing some fruit. What I found exceeded all expectations.

Almost all the trees were supporting generous numbers of shaggy-capped acorns. One specimen was even holding a few weather-darkened caps from the previous year. Acorns two years in a row are almost unheard of with most native oaks!

My reasons for excitement were not confined to this species' productiveness. What was most encouraging is that this was all happening on some very infertile surface-mine soil. I managed to make some other observations of notable importance. Some trees were protected from deer by wire cages, and some had no protection at all. The unprotected trees showed almost no evidence of deer browsing. In this same region, most native oak seedlings struggled just to survive.

On a hunting trip to Ohio, I was fortunate to have an opportunity to observe the progress of a large-scale oak planting. The red, scarlet, and chestnut oaks were all suppressed by deer browsing. Most of them had their work cut out for them just to rise above the whitetail. I am certain that many will not survive.

The burr oaks were faring much better. They did show signs of browse damage, but it was limited, and their prospects for survival looked good. The young sawtooth oaks in this same planting were by far the largest of all the oak species. Almost all were too tall to be affected by deer and showed next to no damage from browsing. It all seemed too good to be true.

The sawtooth oak at (L) is nutrient-deprived. The tree at (R) is growing with autumn olive and is benefitting from the nitrogen that the olive tree's roots produce. Note the color and leaf size differences.

On the previous strip mine site, some of the oaks were interplanted with autumn olive. Most of the sawtooths that were growing next to autumn olive bushes were almost double the size of the ones that were not. The autumn olives were serving as nurse trees for the oaks, which in turn were obviously benefiting from the nitrogen-fixing abilities of this species. Autumn olive is very shade intolerant, and eventually, the oaks will shade it out. Perhaps if one desires to control the aggressiveness of autumn olive, oak plantings would be more favorable than chemical controls.

My experience with sawtooth oak began about a decade ago. I had an opportunity to chat with Ned Weston, a regional land manager for the Pennsylvania Game Commission at the time. Ned was very high on sawtooth oak. He told me that it was doing very well on some strip mine locations in his region, and it was beginning to reproduce and spread without assistance. Armed with that information, I contacted my friends at the game commission and arranged to have a few seedlings shipped to me.

When the package arrived, they were pretty much what I had expected—small seedlings, each with a short section of huge taproot, typical for a nut-bearing tree. These are noncontrollable factors that make oaks difficult to transplant and slow to establish themselves.

In my backyard nursery, I can grow an apple tree to a height of around six feet in two growing seasons. Expect sawtooth oak to be no more than three feet high at the end of three growing seasons due to transplant shock. With apple, crab apple, and hawthorn, I like working with a tree in the five- to six-foot size.

But with oaks, I want them no more than three feet high. On our oak plantings, I lost some of the largest trees due to transplant shock, while almost all the smaller-sized specimens survived.

I prefer to work with container-grown tree stock. After a couple of years, the roots of the young trees will begin to protrude outside of their containers. On species with large taproots, this is an undesirable condition. Keep the young oaks on the small size, and they will transplant much better.

Sawtooth oak is native to Japan and the Far East. It is somewhat smaller than most native oak species, topping out around fifty feet tall at maturity. Even if you are not a die-hard naturalist, this is an exciting species. Not native, it was introduced from Japan or Asia and is a member of the white oak family.

Sawtooth oak is very productive and bears fruit yearly. The majority of our native oaks only fruit approximately every second or third year. Sawtooth fruits at a young age—five to seven years being the norm. White, red, and black oaks usually need forty years before they produce.

Sawtooths have proven to be one of the most adaptable oaks in existence. They prefer highly acidic soil but will flourish in neutral pH soil as well. Some of the most aggressive growth that I observed on sawtooths was on seedlings planted in to soil so acidic that it would not support grass.

In an area of Ohio where I hunt, I had an opportunity to observe large-scale oak plantings. Of the seven species of young oak seedlings that were planted there, sawtooth was the one that exhibited the least impact from browsing deer. This is significant since deer pose one of the most serious problems to the survival of young oak seedlings.

Is its status as an introduced species a concern? I don't think so. This tree reaches a height of about fifty feet. The majority of our nation's hardwoods top out at eighty to one hundred feet. The taller height of native trees is nearly certain to force sawtooths into the role of subdominant, nonaggressive species.

Chestnut Oak and Chinquapin Oak

Like sawtooth, these two additional species show promise, especially on reclaimed surface mine sites, since they demonstrate tolerance to well-drained soils.

One of the biggest challenges in working on strip mine soils is finding species that can adapt or flourish in very low-moisture conditions. On reclaimed mine sites, the soil and underlying rock have been fragmented to a depth of one hundred feet or more. Water tables that once were close to the surface are now far below where tree roots can penetrate.

Chestnut (rock oak) and Chinquapin are species that have long flourished on those ridgetops that lose moisture rapidly. Again, these are species with which I have only recently worked, but both show promise in these moisture-deprived locations.

Black Locust

Black locust is a widely planted species on reclaimed surface mines to control erosion. It is ideally suited to this purpose. The root system of a locust tree is quite shallow, rarely going deeper than one foot beneath the surface. The roots often extend laterally outward one hundred feet or more from the tree base.

Black locust is a member of the legume family—a family of plants and trees that fix nitrogen into the soil. This feature enables them to thrive in very sterile soils. It also excretes chemicals from its roots that are toxic to many species of plants. Grasses, however, are not affected by these chemicals and have formed a symbiotic (beneficial) relationship with the tree's roots. Grasses thrive on nitrogen clinging to the shallow root system of the tree and grow aggressively due to the lack of competition from other species. Green, lush habitat provides quality brood habitat for turkeys as well as high protein food for deer and elk.

Where heavily planted, black locust usually becomes diseased, and so is a short-lived species. Where lightly intermixed with hardwoods, locust can grow large and exceed a height of 80 feet. Native species are quick to colonize short-lived locust plantings that have fallen victim to insects or disease.

Blackberries and raspberries grow aggressively due to the nitrogen fixed into the soil by the tree roots. The cover that the vigorously growing brambles provide is usually followed by oak and hardwood regeneration—perhaps nature's version of a protective wire cage. Black locust spreads quickly through root rhizomes (root sprouts) from the far-reaching lateral roots. So this species should not be planted near food plots that you desire to maintain as permanent openings.

Black locust has very low value as hardwood but is a premier firewood. Its most redeeming characteristic is that it is an important pioneer species, vital to hardwoods, eventually recolonizing ravaged areas like reclaimed strip mines. The ability of black locust and honey locust to stimulate grass growth and increase forage output, definitely earn them a place in eastern elk management plans.

Honey Locust

This is a tree species best suited to deer management. This species is more long-lived and grows to a larger size than black locust and has proven to be more disease resistant too. It produces a huge seedpod (1 3/4 × 12 long), and pod production is heavy. They are thick, quite sweet, reportedly high in energy and protein, and readily consumed by deer. Although this is a widely adaptable species, its adaptability may be somewhat reduced in elevations above 2,000 feet. Pennsylvania is the extreme northern limit of its range. Like its cousin, the black locust, this tree also spreads by root sprouts and should not be planted near wildlife food plots.

Red Mulberry

It is a large tree that can grow to a height of sixty feet and is a heavy producer of sweet fruit that closely resembles blackberries. Birds, grouse, black bears, and wild turkeys enthusiastically consume the fruit of this tree. The most common species of mulberry produces a heavy crop of fruit about midsummer. Fruit breeders also have developed an ever-bearing mulberry tree that produces fruit throughout the summer. This is a species that prefers moist, well-drained locations. However, I do have some trees planted in soil that is quite acidic, and they are growing well.

Pennsylvania is probably at the northern limit of its species' range. I have some trees planted on exposed ridgetops on the

Allegheny Plateau, and they are somewhat out of their environment. These trees often experience winter dieback and diminished fruit production. When planting mulberry trees, avoid the very highest mountaintops. Also, keep your plantings in sheltered locations to ensure best results.

Insects and diseases cause little impact on mulberry, and even mice are slow to girdle young trees. However, porcupines are a major problem. I have found it to be nearly impossible to keep them from destroying my trees. Groundhogs, if present, will also strip a young tree of its leaves and slow its growth. Porcupines and groundhogs are good climbers, and I have yet to find a way to keep them out of trees. I have tried a three-foot tree protector, and they still manage to climb the tree or the wire cage protector.

If you have porcupines in your area, it would be advisable not to waste your time and money planting mulberry trees. If porkies are rare in your region, mulberry is a great soft mast-producing species to plant in your camp yard. Trust me, the turkeys and birds will find your tree. One word of caution—oxidized iron is very toxic to mulberry. If you use rusted wire to protect your young tree, it will kill them. Use new zinc-coated wire cages to protect your trees.

Mountain Ash

Although native to Pennsylvania, I have observed only a couple of isolated specimens of mountain ash growing in our state. Knowledgeable woodsmen, however, have told me tales of ridgetops in both Centre and Bedford counties that support appreciable numbers of these trees.

Mountain ash has all the characteristics of a tree that is adapted to growing on dry locations such as ridgetops. It is nearly in full leaf by the time our native hardwoods begin to break bud. Aggressive growth begins immediately, and slows before the warmer summer months bring to a complete standstill. From this period on, any nutrients gathered by the tree will go only into producing fruit. In my nursery, after the dog days of summer arrive, you can water it until the cows come home, and it will not grow an inch.

Mountain ash is not a true member of the ash family. It is actually quite closely related to the rose family and is not affected by the emerald ash borer. Pluck a young tree from its growing pot, and you can see where its roots avoid the moister soil close to the bottom of the container. Obviously, this species prefers well-drained soil. I planted my first mountain ash trees to enhance wildlife habitat about seven or eight years ago. I am very impressed with the initial results because these specimens have demonstrated aggressive growth and have produced fruit in their second year after planting. These ash trees also appear to be well adapted to acidic forest soils, and some I have observed are doing well in alkaline soils too.

I wish I could tell you that there are no problems associated with attempting to propagate mountain ash. Unfortunately, like most trees, this one has problems that are unique to the species. If you would like to establish mountain ash plantings, fencing your trees is a must. I expect that heavy foraging by whitetails here in Pennsylvania has suppressed this native specimen to the point of near extinction. Trunk borers are also problematic and will inflict mortality if control measures are not implemented against these pests.

And then there are bears. They can reduce a tree to splinters overnight. Take heart, however, several years ago, an old bruin worked over an Asiatic crab apple planting really badly. I wanted to cry. Two years later, however, these same trees had recovered remarkably well and carried a heavy load of fruit. Always remember that bears will be bears.

The mountain ash trees that are available at your local nursery are probably European mountain ash. I would expect them to produce results similar to our native mountain ash. Trying to determine the difference between these two species is probably splitting hairs. If you must have the native variety, you may consider checking out the game commission website. Their Howard nursery may have some available for purchase.

In the short time that I have worked with mountain ash, I have been impressed with the results. Deer, turkey, grouse, bear, and birds are just a few of the critters that benefit from ash plantings. If you would like to do something good for wildlife, consider planting a couple of these trees in your camp yard. Also, remember to plant where trees have at least a half day of sunlight.

Apple Choices

Choices—life can be full of them! We live by the choices we make, and we can die by them too. If we make mostly good choices, life can be quite rewarding. If our choices are questionable, satisfaction can be elusive. It is a very similar circumstance when we are developing a wildlife habitat enhancement plan. Match the shrub or tree in a planting to the proper environment, and it will likely reward us with a lifetime of satisfaction.

When planting apple trees, things can be a bit more complex. With apples, species selection can be the difference between success and failure. Unfortunately, the majority of apple cultivars that are available at our local lawn and garden centers are poor choices for wildlife habitat improvement efforts. Macintosh, Yellow Delicious, and Stayman have very poor resistance to apple scab, and Red Delicious trees develop flawed limb structure. Do you think limb structure is not important? Tell me that after a 350-pound bear has done some chin-ups on a limb already heavy with apples.

If you are to have a total understanding of the negative effects of apple scab, you must learn to identify it and know how it works. Apple scab is a fungus and a member of the mold family. It usually makes its first appearance about the same time your fruit trees are breaking blossom. If present, it will be visible on the upper surfaces of an infected apple leaf and will appear as yellowish-green spots or splotches. These discolorations will eventually turn brown, and if the infection is severe enough, it will cause the tree to purge all infected and damaged leaves. This same fungus will also show up on the young, tender stems of developing fruit and will look like rust-like watermarks.

At this point, the fruit tree will purge all infected fruit. Scab outbreaks will be especially bad in the damp, cool weather conditions common to Pennsylvania. One September, a hunting buddy and I were scouting for deer when we dropped in on an old apple orchard to check for apples. Where air circulation was good and dampness was less of a factor, a few trees were carrying a heavy load of fruit, and deer sign was evident. Where air circulation was poor, however, trees were almost leaf-free, and had no fruit to offer—victims of an apple scab outbreak.

These same trees will not produce fruit the following year because scab lesions damaged the foliage and caused these trees to purge their leaves. Without leaves, photosynthesis cannot take place, and the tree cannot store or produce enough starches and carbohydrates to create a future crop of fruit. It is doubtful they will even produce any blossoms the next year because their "onboard computers" know that they have not manufactured and stored enough energy to make fruit. It may take several years of near-perfect, low-moisture conditions, a rarity in the Northeast before they will bear fruit again.

In commercial orchards, apple scab is a controllable problem. Commercially grown apples are sprayed with pesticides almost weekly. The supervisor simply adds a fungicide to the mix, and the problem is solved. Spraying fruit trees, especially large mature trees that have been planted for wildlife, ranges from impractical to nearly impossible. What is a hunter to do? Actually, the answer is not all that complicated—plant disease-resistant cultivars. Most commercial nurseries offer disease-resistant strains of apples.

Although the fruit they produce may be of a slightly lower quality than most commercial varieties, this becomes a nonfactor to the less demanding palates of wildlife.

Fruit tree breeders have developed disease-resistant strains of apples by crossbreeding apples with Siberian crab apples. Species that have good disease resistance are Liberty, Macfree, Johnafree, Prima, Prescilla, Enterprise, and Goldrush. In my backyard orchards, York

Imperial, Golden Russett, and Fireside have shown reasonable resistance to scab and would be good choices as well.

As much as I like apples, I am forced to admit that crab apples may be a better choice to plant, especially if we are targeting wild turkeys. Crabs tend to be very disease resistant, productive, and hardy. Good species to plant are Dolgo, Indian Magic, Sargent, and Professor Springer. Asiatic crab apples (distributed by the Pennsylvania Game Commission) are as hardy, disease-resistant, and productive as they come.

Don't rule out Washington hawthorn. Although it is not an apple, it is one tough, productive, and disease-resistant little tree with excellent fruit-retention characteristics. Some varieties of apples tend to be biennial producers. Plant multiple cultivars, and you greatly improve the likelihood of having an annual crop of fruit. Be aware as well that like species of apples will not cross-pollinate. Plant two or more cultivars to ensure good pollination.

Always select standard stock over dwarf or semidwarf stock. Dwarf and semidwarf trees are grafted to nonaggressive roost stocks and are not intended to be free-standing trees. In orchards, controlled-sized trees are staked or trellised to provide additional support.

Under professionally controlled conditions, some dwarfs will out produce standard stock trees. However, it does require a greater number of trees per acre under highly professional care to achieve these results. In our backyards, or on State Game Lands, standard-sized trees will produce better results. Morse, Stark Brothers, and South Meadows nurseries are good sources of disease-resistant cultivars. If you cannot find standard trees, plant your stock deeper than where the graft union took place, usually 4–12 inches above ground level. Your semidwarf will then develop into a standard-size tree with a well-anchored root system.

Approach your wildlife enhancement projects with a well-thought-out plan, and your efforts will be rewarded. Get it right, and your project will produce fruit for decades. Sometimes, success can be as simple as a species selection.

Pear Choices

"Hey, Joe, I planted some pear trees, and they all died. What happened to them?"

My usual response is "Let me guess, you probably planted Bartlett or Bosc, didn't you?" A nod of the head usually confirms my suspicions.

For people who work with pear trees, it is common knowledge that these species are all highly susceptible to the fire blight—a disease that is usually fatal to young, infected trees. And like apple tree stock, species of pear stock prompted or promoted by local lawn and garden centers are usually poor choices for wildlife enhancement projects. Once again, it will be necessary to resort to mail-order nurseries to better satisfy your needs.

When selecting pear cultivars as a food source for wildlife, it is an absolute necessity that your choices are varieties which are highly resistant to fire blight. So what is fire blight? How do you recognize its presence, and what can be done to control it?

Fire blight is a bacterial infection that usually makes its appearance after a young fruit tree makes an aggressive new growth spurt. It enters the tree through this new tender tissue at the branch tip. The first sign of fire blight is that the infected tip appears wilted. Within days, the branch will take on a scorched or blackened look, thus the name "fire blight."

When this deadly disease is detected, all infected tissue must be removed immediately. Examine the branches closely, looking for caramel-colored streaks in the bark. Cut off that branch twelve to fifteen inches beyond the last visible sign of infection. On a young tree, you may have to remove more than half of the tree. Take note, if you skimp, you lose!

Remember to disinfect all contaminated pruning tools to prevent spreading the disease. A mixture of one-third Clorox bleach and two-thirds water will serve as a disinfectant. A pump spray Windex-style bottle will serve as a perfect applicator. Fungicides and insecticides are completely ineffective against fire blight. Until recently, the only known control was composed of a mixture of hydrated lime and Bordeaux powder. The most practical way to control fire blight is to plant cultivars that are resistant to this virus.

GioVan, Trophy, Doc's Special, Starking Delicious, Drippin' Honey, and Kieffer are species I do recommend. Kieffer is a very bland-tasting pear, so I do not recommend it for home use. However, it is very hardy, productive, and adaptable, and wildlife will readily consume it. Also, I planted Moonglow (a supposedly blight-resistant species) in my home orchard. Unfortunately, I had so many blight issues with this tree that I eventually cut it down.

In recent years, there has been considerable interest in pears as a wildlife food source, and this newfound excitement may be quite justified. Pear trees are almost immune to foliage diseases that are so problematic with apple trees. They also exhibit better resistance to insects as well and grow aggressively, even in poor soils.

You are now probably asking yourself, "What should I plant, pears or apples?" I would highly recommend your habitat enhancement efforts include a mixture of apple, pear, and crab apples. You should consider throwing a few Washington hawthorns into the mix.

By combining different tree species, you increase disease and insect resistance. Of almost equal importance is the fact that the bloom time of these mixed cultivars will occur at different times. This makes it less likely for frost or freezes to eliminate your entire fruit crop, thereby ensuring the critters will have something to eat. Apple trees are also slightly susceptible to fire blight, and on a rare occasion, I will lose a tree. Fortunately, the disease-resistant varieties that I recommended in "Choices, part 1" are also very blight resistant.

When blight is detected on a large, mature fruit tree, it seldom creates a serious problem. Usually, the infection kills only a small fruiting branch (fruit spur) and rarely will it destroy a large scaffold limb. On a young tree, the disease is almost always fatal if corrective action is not immediate.

There are many apple cultivars that will perform satisfactorily at providing food for wildlife. With pears, however, the choices are more limited, and the consequences of a bad choice are much more dramatic. And you will have to choose at least two different varieties of pears or apples to ensure proper cross-pollination since like varieties will not cross-pollinate. With both pears and apples, species selection can be the difference between success and failure. Do your homework before you plant, and you can be certain that the results will be much more rewarding.

Evergreens: Thermal Cover

A bout of cabin fever drove me out of the house to see what was going on in the woods with the turkeys. I drove to one of my favorite hunting locations and started looking for tracks in an effort to find the birds. I found an abundance of food sources but no turkeys and no tracks. Rose hips and crab apples surrounded the perimeter of the food plots. Why were there no turkeys here?

I suspected the complete absence of thermal covers was to blame. Lesson learned! For wildlife to utilize food sources, thermal cover must not be far away. Thermal cover is often one of the most overlooked components of wildlife habitat. The term "thermal cover" almost always refers to conifer trees or pine and spruce plantings. Winter temperatures beneath conifers often average five to seven degrees Fahrenheit warmer than under surrounding hardwoods, and wind chills are greatly reduced as well.

In frigid temperatures, birds and animals hemorrhage calories at an alarming rate. Burning calories faster than they can be replaced— death usually follows. No bird or animal wants to spend a night in an open, windswept location. Reducing exposure to the elements greatly enhances an animal's chance of survival and diminishes wind chill significantly. Some wildlife biologists believe that 10 percent of our forests should be composed of conifers.

Conifer Selection

There is simply no "best species" of conifer. The trick is to find varieties that best adapt to the conditions that are present at the planting site you have selected. Also note this, a growing movement of people are reluctant to accept planting any non-native species for fear these introductions will become aggressive and displace native species.

When it comes to conifers, the fear is unsubstantiated. Our native species—white pine, hemlock, and white spruce—are shade-tolerant and can compete in hardwood forests. Almost all our alien species of conifers are very shade intolerant and cannot compete with native species. They must have almost complete exposure to the sun in order to survive and reproduce. With the hemlock adelgid (a fatal tree pest infestation) devastating our native hemlock stands, planting some non-native conifers may be the equivalent of throwing a lifeline to wildlife.

A Look at Our Options

White Pine

White pine is a fine native species that has proven to be quite adaptable to a wide range of conditions and soil types. It can be found growing on high ridgetops, floodplains, and any place in between. White pines have proven to produce high-quality softwood and develop into a reasonably disease resistant, very large, long-lived tree.

One negative aspect of this species is its vulnerability to browsing by deer. With conifers, a food rule of thumb to remember is this, the shorter and stiffer the needle, the more resistant it is to browsing. When planting white pines, it is advisable to include some more browse-resistant species in your plan. If the deer take your white pine down, you will still have something left to produce shelter.

Scotch Pine

As much as I prefer diversity, this is a species on which you would be wise to pass. It has very little resistance to disease, has rather sparse foliage, is highly susceptible to porcupine damage, seldom grows to large size, and tends to be short-lived (usually less than twenty-five years). Enough said!

Red and Austrian Pine

I chose to group these two species together because they are almost identical in appearance and habitat requirements. Both need nearly total exposure to sunlight and well-drained soil to survive. Both species are widely planted on reclaimed strip mines and are a great source of pulpwood. These species produce long, stiff needles that are somewhat resistant to deer-browse damage. Both species are reasonably disease resistant and moderately vulnerable to damage and mortality from porcupines.

Eastern Hemlock

This soft, short-needled native species is most often found growing in acidic soil in cool valleys and ravines, especially on the north side of ridges. They are very adaptable to poorly drained locations and bottomlands. Deer often forage heavily on hemlock during periods of heavy snow, and its foliage contains 17 percent protein. But hemlocks are under attack from the woolly adelgid, and until we see how this scenario plays out (and it doesn't look good), I think we would be advised to take a wait-and-see attitude before planting hemlocks.

Red and White Spruce

These are two species with very similar characteristics. Both are widely adaptable to many soil types, and both are quite tolerant of shade. The two tend to be somewhat slow-growing but produce dense thermal cover, making them an ideal choice for shelterbelt plantings for deer, grouse, and turkeys. All spruce species tend to be less vulnerable to porcupine damage than the pine group and are seldom browsed by deer.

Norway Spruce

Yes, this is an alien species. But it is hard for me not to get excited about it. Norways do best in moist soil but also adapt to porous, well-drained strip mine soils. Among the pine and spruce species, it is probably the fastest-growing of all. Sometimes, growth of two feet or more per year is common. Norways are shade-intolerant, and natural reproduction of this species is quite rare—factors that should appeal to the naturalist. Norways develop into a very large, long-lived tree. Plant the species, along with other pines and spruces, for best results.

European Larch

This is a deciduous conifer-type tree that purges its needles yearly. It favors moist soil but adapts to rocky strip mine substrate quite well. Natural reproduction on barren soil is quite common with this species. It develops into a large, straight tree quite rapidly and is highly marketable for pulpwood and framing lumber.

Larch has a place in large-scale pine plantings. It does not provide great thermal cover, but its casting of needles on a yearly basis helps develop topsoil on sterile strip mine subsoil. It also has a light overhead canopy. Often, we find native species such as white pine, hemlock, and blackberry growing under its overstory. However, larch is very shade intolerant. If you plant this species, be certain to establish some pine or spruce planting nearby for thermal cover.

Blue Spruce

Blue spruce is a beautiful tree that is well adapted to dry upland locations and reclaimed strip mines. Blues are shade intolerant and grow slower than many others in the conifer group. On the positive side, they are blessed with a dense canopy that provides excellent thermal cover, and they resist disease well. Most importantly, this is probably the least impacted of the conifer group by porcupine foraging.

If you are a naturalist, take comfort in the fact that I have never witnessed natural regeneration by blue spruce in Pennsylvania. I am certain they can reproduce here, but apparently, the conditions necessary for their natural reproduction seldom exist in eastern hardwood forests. As always, in large pine plantings, it would be wise to mix multiple species types in order to increase tree diversity and disease resistance. That way, you are not placing all your eggs in one basket. Lose one species to disease or insect infestation, and you will have others left to provide shelter and cover.

May all your efforts bear fruit!

Planting and Maintenance

GROW YOUR OWN

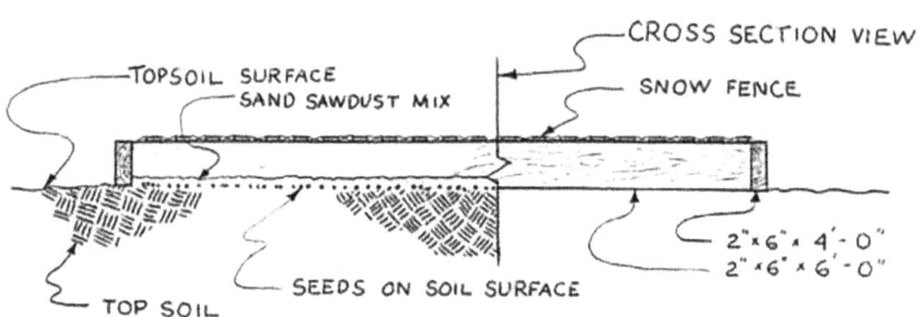

STEPS TO SUCCESS

1. SELECT A GOOD PLANTING LOCATION – CHOOSE AN AREA IN YOUR GARDEN WHICH IS NOT CONTAMINATED WITH WEED SEED. REMOVE <u>ALL</u> WEED ROOTS WITH A GARDEN SPADE. IF A SODDED AREA IS TO BE USED, COVER IT WITH BLACK PLASTIC SHEET ABOUT THREE MONTHS BEFORE PLANTING DATE. TO KILL GRASS OR WEEDS. PLACE PLENTY OF STONES ON PLASTIC TO SECURE.
2. TILL SOIL – <u>AFTER</u> ALL WEED ROOTS HAVE BEEN REMOVED. IF SOIL IS CLAY TYPE OR EXCESSIVELY SANDY, ADD SOME WELL ROTTED SAWDUST OR PEAT MOSS. ALSO ADD ABOUT 1 LB. 10-10-10 FERTILIZER AND SOME LIME.
3. TREAD SOIL UNTIL FIRM – A HARD BOTTOM PAIR SHOES WORKS BEST. DON'T PACK SOIL TOO HARD. YOU SHOULD BE ABLE TO SEE BOOT PRINTS.

4. PLACE 2" x 6" x 4' x 8' WOOD FRAME IN PROPER LOCATION – FRAME SHOULD BE POSITIONED SO THAT WHEN SNOW FENCE IS ATTACHED LATTICE STRIPS RUN IN A NORTH-SOUTH DIRECTION.
5. PLANT SEEDS – SEEDS OR BERRIES SHOULD BE PLANTED AROUND THANKSGIVING DAY; EARLIER IF WINTER STORMS THREATEN; LATER IF CONDITIONS ARE MILD.
6. COVER SEEDS – SEEDS SHOULD BE COVERED WITH ABOUT 1" OF SAND SAWDUST MIXTURE. USE ABOUT THREE SHOVELS OF <u>DARK WELL ROTTED</u> SAWDUST TO ONE SHOVEL OF SAND. (EACH SEEDLING WILL NEED ABOUT $1\frac{1}{2}$"-2" GROWING SPACE)
7. ATTACH SNOW FENCE – USE ABOUT 6 ROOF NAILS TO SECURE TO FRAME.
8. WATER OCCASIONALLY – ONLY IF DRY CONDITIONS EXIST.
9. WEED OFTEN – WEEDS SHOULD <u>NOT BE ALOWED</u> TO GROW TALLER THAN PLANTS.

SPECIAL NOTES: IF POSSIBLE, PLANT BERRIES THE DAY THEY ARE PICKED. IF YOU WANT TO STORE THEM SEVERAL DAYS, SPREAD ON CARDBOARD IN A COOL PLACE.

PEATMOSS CAN BE SUBSTITUTED FOR SAWDUST

IF MICE WORK SEED BEDS, SEEDS CAN BE ARTIFICIALLY STRATIFIED AND PLANTED IN THE SPRING.

Tree Plantings: A Vision for the Future

It is not uncommon to observe tree plantings or food-plot establishments never reaching their maximum potential because the project coordinator lacked vision. I recently saw a classic example of such a lack of foresight. On a reclaimed strip mine, a project supervisor planted four rows of Washington hawthorn, and the young trees were carrying a good crop of fruit. Unfortunately, Norway spruce were planted on both sides of the hawthorn. This created a problem. The slow-growing hawthorns—which rarely grow to a height of thirty feet—were quickly being overtaken by the fast-growing Norways, which grow to a height of eighty feet or more. I expect that the small hawthorns will produce fruit for only several more years before being shaded out by the fast-growing conifers.

A great fruit-holding species like Washington hawthorn planted beside spruce to provide winter thermal cover was a great plan. However, the project originator lacked the ability to see fourteen years into the future. Had he developed a plan that did not deny the hawthorn's sunlight, his project would have had tremendous long-term potential for wildlife.

Another common mistake I often witness with fruit tree plantings is that trees are planted too close to the perimeter of the herbaceous openings. On newly established food plots, limbs from the surrounding trees have not had sufficient time to develop lateral growth. A young shrub planted thirty feet from the outer edge of your food plot looks as if it has plenty of space to develop. But after the surrounding forest puts on thirty feet of lateral growth, a different picture emerges. Your fruit trees now have turned into leaners—a condition that is eventually fatal to the tree.

Fruit trees planted too close to the woods almost always develop into "leaners" with out-of-balance fruit loads. Leaners usually topple as they approach peak-bearing years.

Initially, after trees have been planted, the layout looks quite good. Observe this same project a couple of decades later, and the project coordinator's expertise-level becomes quite obvious. Remember, tree and shrub plantings are labor-intensive and expensive. Take time to sit down and visualize what you want your project to look like twenty years from now. A little extra preparation can pay dividends for decades.

Trees in a Bucket

Being the proprietor of a small backyard fruit tree nursery—as well as the habitat project coordinator for one of our local chapters—has given me an opportunity to experiment with various techniques of establishing and maintaining fruit trees, which are intended to provide food for wildlife.

In our chapter's first tree-planting attempts, we utilized conventional bare-rooted nursery stock. Although we had reasonably good results, it became obvious that there had to be a better way. For openers, I had problems right in the nursery. Removing fruit trees from the ground with a spade was both frustrating and time-consuming. Regardless of my efforts, it was almost impossible to remove the trees without having them sustain considerable damage to their root systems. When the removal process was completed, the stock had to be quickly packed in a medium—usually rotten sawdust—to prevent the small capillary roots from freezing or drying out.

The problems didn't stop there. Root loss and disturbance usually led to a tree that required plenty of attention and TLC at planting time and for the first year or two in its new environment. Without an occasional watering and regular applications of pesticides, tree mortality became a serious problem—back to the drawing board because there had to be a better system!

This is a portion of my backyard nursery, where thousands of fruit trees have been raised prior to their adoption onto game lands and reclaimed strip mines across Central Pennsylvania. Note how efficiently square buckets—common to cat litter containers—maximize garden space and give the buckets a new lease on life!

After a rare straining of my gray matter, I decided to use five-gallon buckets, first drilling four or five 3/8"—diameter holes in the bottom of each bucket for drainage and then placing a small Asiatic crab apple, Washington hawthorn, or grafted apple tree seedling in each bucket, along with soil, a shot of Miracle-Gro, and water. These buckets were placed in a trench in the nursery, deep enough so that when it was backfilled with topsoil, only two to three inches of each bucket was visible above the ground surface. Nesting the trees down into a protective blanket of topsoil is vital to their survival. Leaving the buckets on top of the ground may seem like an easy solution, but the constant freeze/thaw cycles of northern latitude winters will kill the tree. Even in warmer climates, a bucketed tree left exposed to the sun will be robbed of its water in only a fraction of the time as a tree safely sunk into the ground.

To say that I am satisfied with the results of container-grown nursery stock would be an understatement. After planting the first group of trees grown in containers, the improved results were obvious. All the trees began to grow almost immediately, and the growth was vigorous, improving the stock's endurance against periods of drought and insect attacks. Even better, tree mortality was reduced to almost zero. Talk about gratifying!

If you wish to try this method of growing nursery stock, there are several things that you should be aware of. First, your seedlings should be planted where a source of water is readily available. The containers in which the trees are planted will be subject to increased capillary action. This is the process by which the sun draws water deep in the soil up toward the surface. Simply put, plants grown in any container will dry out quickly if not watered regularly.

During periods of reduced rainfall, it will be necessary to give each tree about one gallon of water at least once a week if good growth is to be sustained. A shot of water-soluble fertilizer every three to four weeks is also a good idea. I usually allow for a path or walkway between every double row of buckets. This gives me better access to the trees when I want to weed, water, or spray them. I also recommend using a couple of inches of mulch material in each bucket to lessen the drying effects of the sun. Shredded newspaper, rotten sawdust, or peat moss will work well. Mulch will also help control weeds and, therefore, reduce labor requirements. After you are finished adding all the components, the bucket should be filled to within 2 inches of the top. This will allow you some reservoir capacity and will speed up the watering process.

When you are ready to transplant your trees (about two to three years), simply lift the container out of the ground. Taproots will occasionally protrude down through the drain holes—creating an anchoring effect—but a sharp twist of the bucket will usually shear them off and alleviate the problem.

Although my efforts have been directed to growing Asiatic crab apple, Washington hawthorn, and other apple trees, this technique should also work well with other species. Bittersweet, mountain ash, chestnut, and dogwood are excellent species that should adapt well to this process.

If you are one of the dedicated few who enjoy wildlife habitat improvement work, I think you owe it to yourself to give this method a try. If you do, I think you will agree with me that it's hard to beat fruit trees raised in buckets!

Tree Protection Systems

At any attempt to plant a young tree, the first thing it is going to need is a good trunk protector. Avoid the spiral trunk protectors that garden supply catalogs market. They are almost worthless! They offer some protection against rabbits but are useless against mice and meadow voles. Worse yet, if you don't periodically release the tension on them, your trunk protectors will gradually constrict as the tree grows, strangling them to death.

I prefer plastic trunk protectors made from a four-inch smooth wall PVC pipe. Trunk protectors should be cut to about two feet long. If you are in a region where snowfall is light, an eighteen-inch length should be appropriate. I find a table saw useful for cutting vinyl PVC pipe. Remember to make a cut the length of the protector. This will enable you to remove the protector when your tree no longer needs it. Should you be late in performing this task, it will allow the trunk guard to expand as the tree grows.

When you install a tree guard, it is of *utmost importance* that the guard extends about 2 inches below the ground surface. If you set the trunk protector on the surface of the ground, I can almost assure you that a rodent is going to tunnel under it and girdle the young tree. PVC trunk protectors are also very convenient and accommodating when herbicides are used to control ground cover around the tree. You can spray right up to the base of the tree with no fear of accidentally killing the tree through herbicide contact.

Plastic trunk protectors do have one serious drawback—porcupines love to eat them. If you are working in an area where "porkies" are abundant, consider an alternative. I suggest you think about a trunk protector made out of hardware cloth. I once read that an experienced fruit grower clearly stated that this was the only trunk protector he would recommend. I don't know where hardware cloth got its name since it is not cloth at all but rather a tightly woven zinc-coated wire mesh. As youngsters, we referred to it as rabbit wire since it was commonly used on the floors of rabbit pens.

I was reluctant to use trunk guards made of hardware cloth since mice could easily climb them. The few that I have used, however, have worked quite well. For reasons that only a mouse would understand, they don't like to climb them, and it's the only trunk guard I found that a porkie won't eat. However, be mindful when using herbicides near hardware cloth to make certain to avoid contact with the tree trunk. Bump a young tree trunk with herbicides, and you can kiss it goodbye.

I have seen corrugated plastic pipe used as trunk protection, but I don't like it. The problem with a corrugated pipe is that the corrugations in the pipe attract insects in much the same way that a magnet attracts iron filings. Gypsy moths like to lay eggs on the corrugations, and you fight a losing war with insects.

Now that you have provided protection to the young tree trunk, it is time to consider how to protect the top of the tree or the branches. Our local chapter system is currently utilizing an agricultural field fence. We started out using wire cages made with a two- to four-inch weave. The wire worked well but was expensive. The field fence has a more open weave but is much more cost-efficient, and it does a good job. For apple trees, we fashion a circular cage from a four-foot-wide by eight-foot-long section of wire. For species such as Asiatic crab and Washington hawthorn, a seven-foot section of wire is adequate since these species tend to grow more upright.

Make certain that the tighter weave of the wire is at the top of the cage, and the more open weave is nearest to the ground. Deer can and will reach their mouth through the more open weave. Near the ground, this is not a problem. Browsing up high can and will eventually kill the young trees. When you place your protective cage around the tree, secure it in place with two steel stakes. One stake should be as high as the cage. The other stake needs only be high enough to secure the base of the cage to prevent it from rotating. It is also important to keep the cage one foot off the ground. If you set the cage on the ground, the deer can and will reach over the top of the cage and eat the top of the young tree. Place the cage on the surface of the ground, and you are creating a safe house for mice and voles. Keep the cage up a foot, and fox and coyotes will reduce confrontations with rodents.

What about the new wave of plastic tree shelters? Well, I have used them but find there are some serious problems associated with them, and for that reason, I seldom use them. The biggest problem with plastic tree shelters is that bears love to destroy them. It is a fact of life that if a six-year-old boy walks past a water puddle, he is going to tramp in it. Likewise, if a bear walks past a plastic tree shelter, he will destroy it.

You might think that there are not many bears in your region, but if you attempt to use plastic guards, you are going to find that there are bears where you did not think you had bears. My friend, Joe Kruise from Coalport, Pennsylvania, has good luck using plastic tree shelters in bear country. Joe plants a small seedling and then provides it with a plastic tree shelter. He utilizes a metal pole with some tough plastic twine. With the tube anchored in this manner, a bear apparently lacks the extra motivation required to bend the shelter. After the shelter is in place, Joe then places a wire cage around the tree shelter. Problem solved! Old bear now no longer finds crunching a tree protector desirable. I guess it now becomes too much of an effort to him.

After the seedling exits the top of the plastic tree shelter, Joe removes the tube and secures the young whip in the center of the cage with some biodegradable cotton string or cheap twine. This keeps down wind damage and allows the young tree time to stiffen. Much of the fruits of Joe's effort can be viewed on State Game Lands number 120 in southern Clearfield County. This game land has several hundred fruit trees growing on it, many of them as a result of his efforts.

We have also found that plastic-grow tubes or tree shelters tend to attract mice, a condition that nearly always proves fatal to the tree inside. You may not be able to completely eliminate this problem, but we have found that it can be greatly reduced by dropping a couple of mothballs down the mouth of the tube. Mothballs are cheap and easy to use.

When I first began planting trees, we often utilized old snow fence for protection—a practice that I now strongly discouraged. I firmly believe that snow fencing attracts rodents since it provides a form of protection and security from avian predators. So I also encourage you to use metal or stiff fiberglass stakes with all your tree guards. Scrap metal conduit, black iron pipe, snow-fence stakes, and metal reinforcement rods all work quite well. Wood stakes can be used but will frost heave, making them undesirable for most applications.

In conclusion, much of the knowledge I have accumulated was learned the hard way—through trial and error. It required numerous failures and lots of patience from local chapter members who have worked with me. Take the lessons I have shared with you and utilize them on your next habitat project, and I can almost guarantee your efforts will bear fruit!

This is a good-looking apple tree on State Game Lands Number 26 in Blair County, Pennsylvania.

This is an ideal tree protection setup! Buried a few inches into the soil, the cut PVC pipe inhibits mice and rabbits from girdling the tree. Two metal posts or rebar are pounded into the ground approximately 18 inches from the tree. If the spacing of your wire fence is gradated, place the narrower openings at the top of the tree, while the wider gaps benefit from the trunk protector at the bottom. Suspend the wire cage a foot above the ground by weaving it through the metal bars. This not only affords easier removal of grass and weeds beneath the tree— eliminating another safe haven for field mice—but also prevents deer from reaching over the cage and browsing the top of the tree.

Dealing with Insects and Tree Diseases

Should I go with a pesticide control program, or should I avoid it?

Good question. When I first started to plant fruit trees, I leaned toward regular pesticide applications to control pests. In recent years, however, I have distanced myself from the use of insecticides. The problem with pesticides is that there is no one chemical that will be effective against all pests or insects. Pest control has become a science, and there is an endless list of insecticides, each to target a different insect species.

To further complicate matters, the majority of these chemicals kill beneficial (predatory) insects, along with harmful (parasitic) insects. Excluding severe insect outbreaks that are devouring your tree's foliage, I would advise against pesticide use.

Carefully observe your young fruit trees. If insect damage is minimal, refrain from spraying. If the damage is becoming excessive, consider a pesticide application. When dealing with very young trees, if the surrounding grasses are quite tall, grasshoppers can be a problem. However, they are quite easy to control, and most insecticides will quickly eliminate them.

Carbahol (Sevin) is a pesticide that I refrain from using on apple trees. It is affordable, reasonably safe to work with, and kills a broad range of insects. Unfortunately, *Carbahol* also kills beneficial predator mites that feed on parasitic European red mites that suck nutrients from the tree leaves. Without the presence of their natural predator, red mite infestations are difficult to control and severely weaken an otherwise healthy apple tree.

Your best bet is to purchase an over-the-counter fruit tree spray mix at a lawn and garden center. Restrict the use of *Carbahol* to only young hawthorn trees. Avoid the use of other insecticides on this species because it is very sensitive to acid-base sprays, upon which the majority of all pesticides are based. Spray the hawthorn trees with other insecticides, and the majority will severely burn the leaves. Repeat applications will kill hawthorn trees. *Carbahol* will also cause fruit trees to purge significant amounts of fruit. Commercial orchards use it for this purpose when apple trees set too much fruit, and a larger apple size is desired. A very effective insecticide that kills a broad range of insects is Imidan. It is reasonably safe to use and affordable. However, it is acid-based and should not be used on Hawthorn.

Dealing with Trunk Borers

Trunk borers are a wasplike insect that lays its eggs near the base of a young fruit tree. When the eggs hatch the young borers tunnel into the bark of the tree and feed on the inner life-giving cambium layer of the bark, the feeding cycle cuts off the nutrient flow between the shrub's branches and its roots. Death soon follows! Borers are the most difficult tree pest to control, and their presence usually leads to a young tree's death. To further complicate matters, there are several species of this problematic insect, and you will need two different insecticides to control them.

Kinetic and Baseline insecticides mixed at the rate of one tablespoon per gallon of water, along with a wetting agent, assist the spray in clinging to the tree bark. Dawn dish detergent added to the spray mix will work reasonably well as a spray sticker. Unfortunately, both Kinetic and Baseline are extremely toxic and dangerous to work with. You will need to consult someone who has a pesticide application license if you choose this route.

When applying the spray mix to the tree, make certain to drench the trunk from ground level up to where the branches begin. The region near the top of the trunk protector is most critical. Here in Pennsylvania, on the Allegheny Plateau, the trees should be sprayed for trunk borers at the end of May and again during the first week of August. In your state or region, it may be necessary to check with your county's agricultural extension service for proper application times.

Trunk borers usually appear when a tree's trunk approaches one inch in diameter. They will continue to be a concern until the young tree's bark starts to develop (smooth appearance disappears) a scale surface, usually at 5 to 6 inches in diameter. If there has been timber-cutting activity in your area and sapling regeneration is evident, you can be confident that trunk borers are present. If the surrounding forest is composed of mature trees with little to no sapling regeneration and your luck holds, they may not be an issue.

Recently, I have had the opportunity to probe the minds of individuals who have specialized knowledge of dealing with this family of insects. The knowledge they have shared with me gives me hope that there are better methods of limiting trunk borer tree mortality.

One expert that I conversed with proclaimed that trunk borers rarely ever attack healthy trees. Studies indicate that stressed or unhealthy trees emit chemical pheromones. Trunk borers home in on those pheromones to locate and target a tree.

I see evidence to support these observations. On fruit trees to which I applied regular maintenance (lime, fertilizer, vegetation control) losses have been significantly reduced. And then there is the additional benefit of larger trees, with good fruit loads much sooner, and rodent problems are significantly reduced. As a general guideline, fruit trees should receive an application of lime at six-year intervals. Fertilizer should be applied at the rate of about one pound of 10–10–10 per inch of trunk diameter—a good rule of thumb. Fertilize yearly, and skip a year occasionally to eliminate nutrient buildup. Do not overfertilize as this can cause some very serious problems. Apple trees can tolerate fairly acidic soil but do best and are subject to less stress when a soil acidity of 6.5 to 7.0 pH is maintained.

If you only care for a limited number of trees, a manual approach may be your best option. Examine your trees often and be on the lookout for chaff-like (digested bark) sawdust tailings, and bb-sized entrance holes near the bases of your trees, especially close to the ground. If you locate an entrance hole, probe the borer's path with the tip of your pocketknife or a stiff piece of wire. The objective is to puncture the grub and put it out of the tree-killing business.

How much of a problem are trunk borers? For some locations, I have seen tree mortality approaching 100 percent! Yes, they can be managed, but it will require some effort on your part—especially in the first six to eight years of the fruit trees' life. Remember, trees can be replaced, but time can never be replaced. Have a maintenance plan in place.

Regular fertilizer and herbicide applications—coupled with vegetation control—will greatly reduce tree stress and trunk borer problems.

The Mulch Question

Should I mulch around young trees or avoid its use? There are no easy answers.

A formerly mulched apple tree in my orchard, with roots exposed after the mulch deteriorated—a condition which would, in all probability, lead to the death of the tree in an unmanicured environment

Mulching does control vegetation, and its use is beneficial at keeping moisture in the soil. Mulched trees usually grow faster than trees without mulch. Unfortunately, mulching brings with it its own set of problems. Organic mulches attract grubs and earthworms, which are protein and attract mice and voles. When these pests show up, they will kill your trees!

In my backyard orchard, mulch has worked out well around my fruit trees. But the backyard is much different from the backwoods. In my yard, the grass is clipped short and offers rodents almost zero protection from predators. In an unmanaged environment, vegetation is usually rank and attuned toward mice. An approach that works well in the backyard can be a disaster in the "back forty."

Another mulch-related problem caught my eye. After a couple of years, the mulch deteriorated, and many of the trees' roots were partially exposed above ground level. These roots developed in or under the mulch in an effort to retrieve water and nutrients, creating a serious problem. The exposed roots attract rodents quickly, acting as a doorway to your trees' underground root system. The mice will then girdle (remove bark) the roots.

A girdled tree will cling to life for a couple of months. Unfortunately, there is nothing you can do to save the severely damaged tree—lesson learned. If you are hard-pressed to pass on organic mulch, there is an acceptable alternative marble-sized crushed limestone, or better yet, slag if you have access to it. Both help reduces the sun's capillary action, which draws moisture from the soil. Lime will leach from the limestone and micro-nutrients from the slag, which is beneficial to your tree's health. Crushed stone also helps soil retain moisture and discourages mice from digging and finding your tree's roots. Stone scree should be dime-sized or larger.

Watering Your Trees

Watering is very labor-intensive and, in most situations, not necessary. Occasionally, hydrating your tree's root system can be a lifesaver. Each tree should receive three to five gallons of water during a single application. Trees should be watered every week to ten days during periods of limited rainfall.

Timing is Everything

The last splinters of light from the evening Sun were being absorbed by the trailing ridge of the Allegheny Front. My planting crew and I were rushing to plant the last of our soft mast-producing seedlings. I opted to do a quick inspection of my crew's efforts. Unfortunately, I discovered that somebody on the team was planting a dozen or more of the smaller seedlings in fist-sized clusters. Planted so tightly together, crowding seedlings is a wasteful practice.

Yes, their actions frustrated me, but when working with volunteers, it is sometimes best to bite your tongue. I removed the seedling clumps with the intention of returning the following day to plant them myself. Realizing the small seedlings would be smothered out by the thick grass, I planted them in locations where the cover was sparse.

Two years later, I returned for a visual inspection of the site, and what I observed surprised and disappointed me. All of the large, two-year-old seedlings planted in thick grass were dead! A close inspection revealed they had been girdled by mice. The only seedlings that survived were the small ones planted where cover was sparse.

An event that I found frustrating at the time actually turned into a very educational experience. Other shrub plantings in heavy cover produced similar results. Lesson learned: Plant your seedlings before cover becomes rank.

Constant battles with mice and meadow voles have taught me that they need structure to survive. Rodents are on the menu of just about every raptor and animal predator in the neighborhood. If they can't see it, they can't catch it.

Much of my habitat enhancement efforts have taken place on reclaimed surface mines. When utilizing any type of seedling at these locations, it is of extreme importance that stock be planted immediately after grasses and legumes have been seeded. It takes about three years for cover crops to thicken to the point where mice begin to infiltrate and establish their presence. If you incorporated your seedlings into the plan in the early stages, their chances of survival are excellent. If done after cover has become dense, mortality rates skyrocket.

What species of tree or seedlings are vulnerable to mice? Almost anything and everything! I have even observed them girdling wild black cheery seedlings—an incredible fact, since cherry bark and leaves contain enough cyanide to kill cattle whom consume its leaves. (When I was a young boy working on a dairy farm, it was my job to check the pasture after thunderstorms, and remove any downed limbs on which cattle could forage.

When you start to develop observant eyes, it is amazing how seemingly little things take on incredible importance. Yes, timing can be everything!

Seeds or Seedlings?

I have a well-worn planting bar that testifies to the number of seedlings that I have planted. In recent years, I have graduated to utilizing seeds to establish select tree, shrub, and vine species with incredible results. Planting seeds in place of nursery stock is not only more cost-efficient, but it also requires far less sweat and labor.

However, the use of seed is mostly restricted to areas where herbaceous growth has been eliminated and where the soil has been recently worked. Your approach should be to scatter or broadcast seeds or berries on freshly scarified soil, and let the weather and rain do the work for you. Success will greatly depend on your timing. If it rains on your seedbed even one time before you apply the seed, your results will be greatly diminished. A single rain will seal the formerly porous soil and cause your seeds to be exposed on the surface.

Large seeds such as acorns and hickory nuts will probably require hand planting. A mattock or shovel is well suited since you should only cover your acorns with an inch or two of soil. When working on recently reclaimed strip mines, I find it advantageous to plant large seeds immediately after a rain. When soil is soft (and not too rocky), I sometimes use my thumb to press the nuts into the soft ground.

If your planting times are stylized efficiently, expect good results! One year after planting acorns on a reclaimed surface mine, I was able to follow where I walked the previous year by following a seedling trail. Yes, the seedlings were small, but the promise they displayed was huge.

A strong belief in what you are doing can lead to a well-worn planting bar.

Pruning Apple Trees

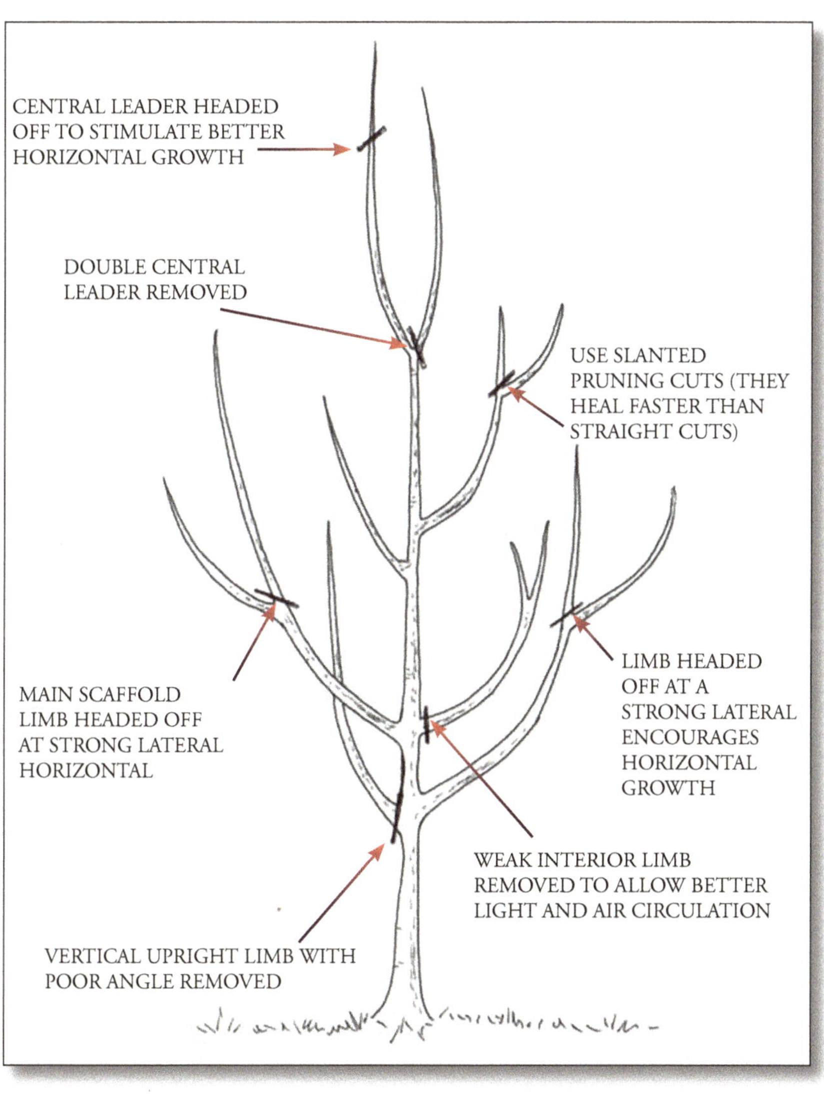

If your goal is to develop healthy, productive fruit trees, it is imperative that you grasp the importance of developing trees with good limb structure. Fruit trees with poor structure rarely produce or carry good fruit loads. Even worse, they are more vulnerable to damage from bears, ice, and the weight of their own fruit.

This is a young apple tree with a double central leader. The leader with the poorer limb structure should be removed.

One of the more commonly observed problems of tree structure—especially with apple trees—is the dreaded "double center." Take care to never let this develop during the pruning process. Trees with this structural fault typically split at the center junction when attempting to support heavy loads (ice, fruit, or bears), with each half splitting and breaking in opposite directions. Even more depressing, it usually happens when your tree is just beginning to approach its peak bearing years.

Every young apple tree should be trained to have one vertical growing branch, called the "central leader." All the main scaffold limbs should extend outward at nearly perpendicular angles from the central trunk leader. It is also advisable not to allow your main scaffold limbs to develop at the same point on the tree trunk. This will cause structural weakness. So allow some space between your limb's anchor points.

Another persistent problem with fruit tree structure is having far too many main scaffold limbs. Your tree should have no more than three to five main branches. Properly spaced limbs with room to correctly develop improved sunlight penetration and better air circulation.

Trees with well-spaced scaffold limbs will produce fruit throughout the interior of the tree.

Air circulation reduces foliage diseases, and sunlight encourages better development of fruiting spurs. Spurs are those short, stubby branches that produce fruit. Limbs void of spurs develop light yields, with fruit being set only at the tips of the branches, resulting in light fruiting. Trees with proper limb structure are low maintenance and generally require only light periodic correction pruning.

Having scaffold limbs anchored to the central trunk leader at the proper angle is very vital. All limbs that grow in upright angles should be removed. Their sharp-angled branches are structurally weak, develop bark inclusions at their anchor points, and will not support heavy fruit loads. You want strong limbs protruding from a central leader as close to perpendicular to the trunk as possible.

Young apple tree with very strong limb structure

The first half-dozen years of a young fruit tree's life are the most important period of its development. If you have done your homework, pruning and training it properly, your tree will develop into a productive specimen, requiring only minimal maintenance and care. When removing limbs, make cuts at the branch's base and take care not to remove the collar *(see diagram)*, which has chemicals that discourage and reduce root rot and bacterial infections.

Clean cuts with minimal wood exposure heal quickly and are less prone to root rot and structural weakness. When removing limbs, the first cut should be an undercut on the limb's underside. Finish the cut from the topside. Undercuts prevent the weight of the limb from causing tears in the tree bark. When shortening a limb, head it off at a strong, horizontal-leading branch, called a lateral branch. If possible, make slant cuts—they heal faster than flat cuts. The branch profile of an apple tree should resemble that of a round-nosed pistol bullet, wider at the bottom and narrowing toward the top.

Before (L) and after (R) pictures of a double center removed from a young apple tree. Note that slant cuts heal much quicker.

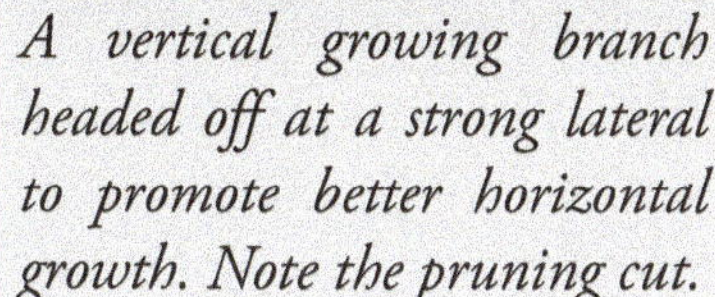

A vertical growing branch headed off at a strong lateral to promote better horizontal growth. Note the pruning cut.

Dotted line illustrates where pruning cut should be made. Collar at the base of the limb should not be removed to minimize wound size. Avoid leaving limb stubs. They inhibit healing, encouraging rot, and disease.

| Horizontal limb development spreads fruit loads over the entire length of the limb, which benefit the structure and longevity of the tree. | Vertical limb development concentrates fruit near the limbs' anchor points, where bark inclusions cause structural weakness, leading to limb breakage. |

Pruning Pear Trees

Pear trees in commercial orchards tend to use the same central leader system that has proven itself so satisfactorily on apple trees. However, some pear growers use pruning techniques that produce trees with different limb structures. These growers allow their trees to develop three or four central leaders. Pear trees with multiple centers tend to better resist fire blight (problematic and almost always fatal on pear) attacks.

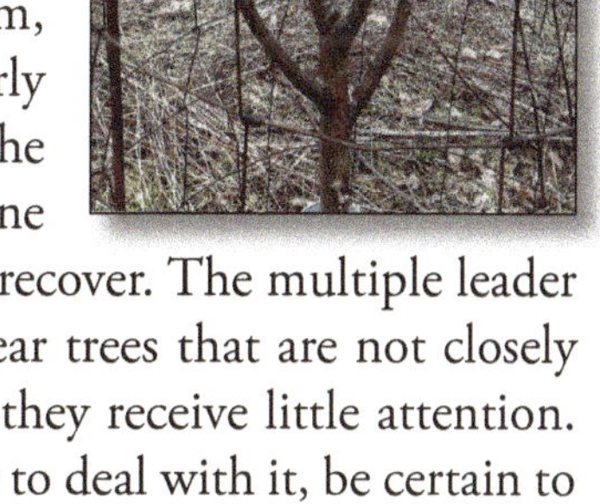

This is a young pear tree with a perfect limb structure. While multiple leaders are discouraged on apple trees, this structure is preferred in pears.

With the central leader system, blight, if not caught quickly, is nearly always fatal to young pear trees. With the multiple leader system, you will lose one or two leaders, and your tree is likely to recover. The multiple leader system is preferable when utilized on pear trees that are not closely monitored, such as trees planted where they receive little attention. To better understand fire blight and how to deal with it, be certain to read "Choices, part 2," in the manual.

Best Time to Prune Fruit Trees

Apple and pear trees can be pruned at any time of year. However, in regions where temperatures can drop to below zero, trees should be pruned during the late dormant period. Where I live in Pennsylvania, I usually start to prune about mid-March. If you do a summer limb removal, be sure to allow your cuts time to heal before the tree enters its dormant period.

Pruning cuts that are exposed to extreme low temperatures (-5 degrees or lower) can result in tissue damage and can cause tree mortality, especially on small trees. Pear trees tend to grow more vertically than apple trees. That needs to be taken into consideration during the pruning process. The multiple central leader system that is suitable for pear trees would be disastrous on apple trees.

Pruning Old, Neglected Apple Trees

The most common problem associated with neglected apple trees is that most have developed far too many limbs. A crowded limb structure usually results in a tree with little to no fruiting wood in the interior of the tree, due to poor sunlight penetration. The end result is a tree capable of producing only a very limited amount of fruit on the outer tips of its branches. Remember, fruiting spurs are those short, stubby branches with abundant leaves. Leaves are important because they produce the sugars and carbohydrates necessary to assist in the development of fruit. It takes the combined efforts of approximately seventeen leaves to produce one apple. The desired effect is quite simple—if you want an abundance of fruit, it is going to take a lot of leaves.

Commercial orchards prune excessively in an effort to increase fruit size for marketability. As a wildlife food source, fruit size is not a factor, and limb removal should be more reserved. The fruit will be smaller, but the yield will be greater. Aggressive limb removal usually causes excessive suckering and increases maintenance requirements.

Unfortunately, the problems associated with neglected trees usually take years to develop and cannot be reversed in a day. Neutralizing the sins of neglect is a process that requires time and some patience. The correct approach to pruning neglected fruit trees is to slowly remove some of the crowded limbs to enable sunlight to reach the interior of the tree. If done slowly, the process will allow the remaining limbs to develop fruiting spurs and greatly improve your tree's health, vigor, and productivity.

The pruning process on old trees should be spread over a period of three to four years. Become too aggressive in your efforts, and at best, you will damage and weaken your tree. At worst, you may kill the tree. Your first actions toward rejuvenating a neglected tree should focus on removing all dead, broken, and diseased branches. Other candidates for elimination are those limbs that protrude from the central (vertical center of the tree) leader at tight, upright angles, limbs that rub other limbs, and those that grow inward toward the center of the tree.

One of the most common mistakes I have observed in the pruning process is the removal of the tree's central leader. This is a mistake that will greatly weaken the tree's structure. It also encourages an excessive number of water sprouts (commonly called suckers) and makes the exposed limbs vulnerable to sunscald and tissue damage.

Your overall objective in dealing with old, neglected trees is to very gradually open them up through limb removal in order to allow the remaining limbs to develop fruiting spurs and better air circulation (decreasing foliage diseases) throughout the tree. If patience and thought are utilized in the pruning process, it can greatly increase the health, productivity, and life span of a long-neglected tree. Remember, too, that herbicide application around a tree—to control competing vegetation—and an application of fertilizer will greatly enhance your tree's health and productivity considerably.

Converting Wild Apple and Wild Pear Trees into More Productive and Disease-Resistant Cultivars

Seed-grown fruit trees seldom develop into highly productive trees. Fruit sets on these trees are light, fruit quality is poor, and production is inconsistent at best. With minimal effort and a little acquired knowledge, young wild apple and wild pear trees can easily be grafted and converted to productive disease-resistant commercial varieties. Grafting is the process of cloning a more productive tree, which eliminates the negative characteristics of the mother stock, and incorporates the positive aspects of grafted stock.

Domestic pear five years after grafting on established Callery pear trees; tree growing on unfertilized strip mine soil

Young, small fruit trees—especially Callery pear—can be found colonizing reverting agricultural land and reclaimed surface mine sites. These trees have tremendous potential if we seize the opportunity. The first step in the conversion process is to seek out young trees of ideal size with which to work. I prefer a tree that has a trunk diameter of one to three inches at shoulder height. Using a small folding saw, such as those used by archers to clear shooting lanes, head the tree off at shoulder height. You want to do the grafting at the height of five feet or more to ensure that deer cannot eat your grafts. Trust me, if they can eat them, they will.

The heading process should be done early to mid-April. After the target tree has been headed, do not remove any of the limbs from the tree at this time. Limbs will be gradually removed later in the process. The newly headed tree will develop numerous whips at the heading sites. Allow these whips to develop freely in the first year. The following spring, before the buds open, select two to four pencil-sized diameter whips to be grafted, and then remove those remaining ungrafted whips.

Domestic pear three months after being grafted on Callery pear

After the tree has been grafted, it is vital that you perform periodic maintenance on it. The first maintenance step should be done for about two months (midsummer) after the grafting took place. All ungrafted suckers that develop in the area of the graft must be removed. This is also the optimum time to remove a couple of the limbs below the grafts on the tree. This will allow more energy to be pushed into the grafts. The remaining ungrafted limbs should be removed gradually over a two- or three-year period.

Remember, removing too many limbs too soon can shock the tree and reduce its health and vigor.

Domestic pear one year after being grafted on an existing calleryana *(Callery) pear tree (my assistant, Bill Weakland, present for size comparisons)*

On newly grafted trees, it is not unusual for the grafts to grow three to seven feet during the first summer! I have some grafted trees that have reached a height of nineteen feet in only three years. Many of these trees produced fruit in the second year after having been grafted! On the more aggressive growing grafts, it may be necessary to head back new growth by 30 percent to stiffen the tree and prevent it from becoming too lanky with drooping branches.

If one is in need of incentive for pursuing these efforts, he needs only to look at the advantages:

    a.   You don't have to purchase a tree.
    b.   You won't need a protective wire cage.
    c.   You don't have to plant a tree.
    d.   You won't need a trunk protector.
    e.   Trunk borers will not be a problem.
    f.   Little need to control vegetation around the tree.
    g.   The tree should be producing reasonable amounts of fruit in three or four years.

Now that I have your attention, it is time to look at the grafting process.

Why do we graft, you may ask? Every apple tree that you purchase has been grafted. It has been estimated that from trees grown from seed, only one of several hundred trees would be capable of producing marketable quality fruit.

In order for a blossom to be pollinated, it must have contact with pollen from another species of apple or pear, since a cultivar cannot pollinate itself. In the cross-pollination process, the only thing that can be guaranteed is that the fruit from seed-grown trees will have little resemblance to the fruit of the parent tree. Trees that grew from seed also have one thing in common—they almost always lack disease resistance. If you want disease-resistant trees that abundantly produce quality fruit, you must graft.

Grafting Fruit Trees

There are many types of grafts, and I will not attempt to cover all these various techniques here. I will focus specifically on the whip graft. Whip grafting will give you a tree a year sooner than most grafts and, in my experience, is one of the simplest grafts to execute. The majority of other grafts require the use of grafting wax. This wax mixture is time-consuming and hard with which to work. Whip grafting is usually done on very young, pencil-diameter trees called whips. Deviate in size very far in either direction, and the grafting process becomes increasingly more difficult.

The first and most important step in preparing to graft is to select good grafting wood (scion wood) from the tree from which you want to graft. Select healthy, straight water sprouts (wrongly called suckers) with good, well-developed buds. The middle third of this whip is where you will harvest your scion wood. The wood from the thin end of the whip has well-developed buds, but it is thin and difficult with which to work. Wood near the thick end of the whip will have small, poorly developed buds that are hard for the rootstock to force open.

To perform a whip graft, closely match the diameter of the scion wood to the young whip (rootstock) to which you want to graft it. Your scion wood should have one to no more than three well-developed buds. Be certain that your utility knife has a new, razor-sharp blade. On both the scion wood and whip, you have to make identical, matching, smooth diagonal cuts about one-and-a-half-inch long each.

After the cuts have been made, approximately one-third of the distance from the toe of each cut, make a cut (with the grain) about half-inch long. The two parts (whip and scion) are slipped together and tightly wrapped with electrical tape. I recommend using a brightly colored tape on your grafts. This is helpful in visually identifying where you made the graft. Remember, grafts are like people. The ones that are not wrapped tightly seldom succeed!

After the grafts start to grow and the new shoots toughen and become woody, use a sharp utility knife and remove all but one of the new shoots. This will become the trunk of the new fruit tree. Usually, about midsummer, I remove the grafting tape. This process, even when done gently, will remove the outer layer of tissue from the tree's bark. This will appear as serious damage, but don't be alarmed. The cambium layer of the bark has not been affected, and the tree will heal quickly.

I have not attempted this, but I have every reason to believe that whip grafting can be successfully completed on wild chestnut stump regeneration. There is a huge root system there just waiting for a disease-resistant graft for that new tree! Before you attempt any new grafts, practice on some whips until you feel comfortable and ready to graft. Grafting is not rocket science. It has been around for at least two thousand years. A friend who never grafted before sat down with me as we grafted one hundred pieces of the rootstock. In the months that followed, only three or four of those grafts did not succeed.

Again, it is important to understand that all grafting must be done in the very early spring before the tree's buds begin to open. In my region of Pennsylvania, I usually graft in late March or the first week of April. And it goes without saying, "Never attempt to graft apple to pear stock or vice versa!"

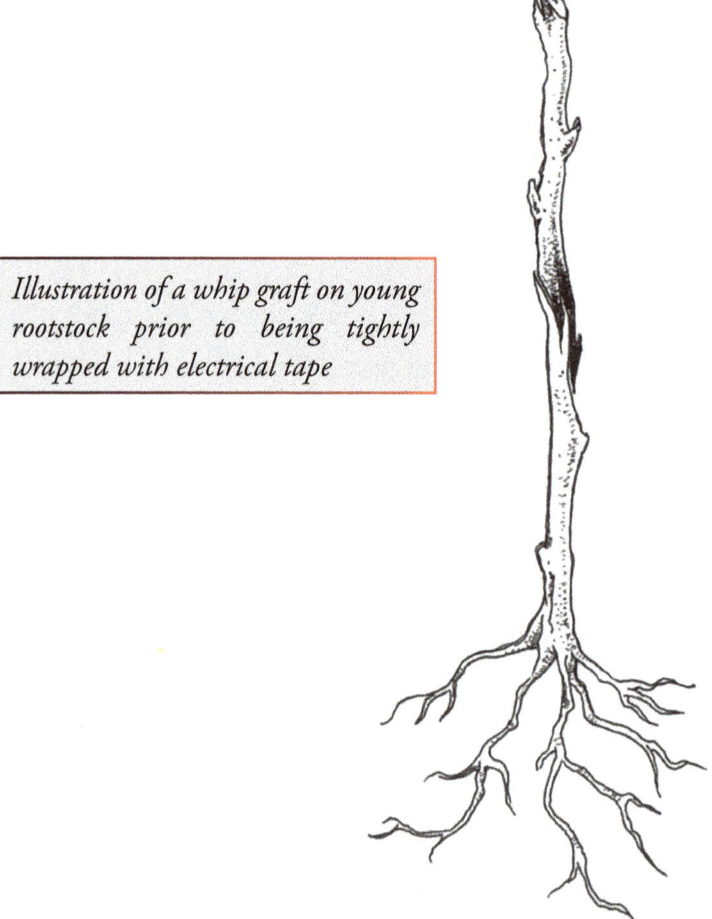

Illustration of a whip graft on young rootstock prior to being tightly wrapped with electrical tape

The Carbohydrate Factor

In the lunchroom at work, several hunters were discussing the heavy acorn crop in the area they hunt. One hunter concluded that this was an indication that we were in for a really tough winter. Finding it difficult to remain on the sidelines of the conversation, I questioned my colleague.

"I am hunting only about fifteen miles from you, and we don't have any acorns. Does that mean your winter is going to be harsh and our winter will be mild?" I asked. My friend glared at me and failed to come up with a response. I expect that in the back of his mind, he was saying not so nice things about me.

And then there was the fellow who told me about the woolly worm that he saw that was all black. Its presence confirmed to him that we were in for a really bad winter. I usually responded by telling him about the woolly worm I just saw that was almost entirely brown in color. I followed by asking my friend if that means that on his side of the highway, they would see a hard winter, but on my side, conditions would be mild. Another nasty glare.

Rather than calling attention to my questionable people skills, perhaps a short, educational course on the subject would be appropriate. Current mast crops are no indication of what future weather conditions will be. They can, however, be a direct result of past weather conditions. In order for a tree to produce fruit (or seed), it must store an ample amount of carbohydrates, starches, and sugars. It takes favorable conditions for this process to take place. The starches are then stored in the trees, twigs, roots, and branches.

After the tree stores enough carbs, it knows it is in condition to produce a crop of fruit and sets an abundance of blossoms. A good mast crop usually follows if the blossoms escape any late frost. After the tree purges its fruit, it has most likely been depleted of carbohydrates and energy. This same tree will go back to storing energy in the form of sugar and starches and is not likely to produce another crop of fruit for a couple more years.

In orchards, fruit farmers rarely experience a year without fruit on their trees. That's because they spend a lot of time and energy fertilizing, liming, pruning, and irrigating their orchard. A wild apple tree of questionable genetics—growing on the next ridge in infertile soil—may produce a crop of apples only once every eight or ten years.

How can this knowledge be of any avail to a hunter, aside from avoiding nasty glares? It would be wise to take a few lessons from the guy who operates the orchard. Pruning that old apple tree where you bushwhacked several bucks over the years would help boost its productiveness. Also, take time to remove any competing vegetation which robs the tree of water and nutrients.

Asiatic crab apple one year after receiving an application of fertilizer

Speaking of nutrients, don't forget about fertilizer. A good rule of thumb is to add about one pound of fertilizer (10–10–10) for each inch of trunk diameter. Do not—and I repeat—do not exceed this amount! Excessive nutrient levels can severely damage the tree. About every third year, I recommend skipping the fertilizer to avoid nutrient buildup. Better to err on the side of safety. If soil is acidic, a coat of lime once every six or seven years would be beneficial as well. The same type of care to that big oak tree will greatly enhance its productivity as well. Skip the lime for this big boy because oaks prefer acidic soils.

Good luck with your newfound knowledge!

Fruit Tree Maintenance

Perhaps you recently planted some fruit trees on your latest habitat improvement project, and now you want to simply relax and wait for them to start producing fruit.

If this is your attitude, you lack experience in this business. To a considerable degree, your success will greatly depend on periodic inspections and routine maintenance of your young trees. If I had a choice of planting ten trees and providing follow-up care or planting one hundred trees and just walking away, my prediction is that the routinely maintained trees will give you superior results.

Of utmost importance is keeping a vegetation-free zone at least six feet in diameter around the base of your young trees. Continue this practice until your trees start to develop a bark scale. This usually happens when the tree trunk reaches five to six inches in diameter.

The purpose of eliminating vegetation is twofold. First, you are removing the other species that compete with the tree for nutrients and water. Second, and most importantly, this will keep mice and voles away from your tree. A rodent guard is part of the solution, and vegetation control completes the plan.

When you occupy the top spot on the menu of just about every predator in the country, you need plenty of cover to survive and hide your movements. Eliminate the protection, and you eliminate most of the problems associated with rodents.

Do not be so naive as to think that a good rodent guard will solve all your problems. If these small packages of destruction burrow down to the tree's roots, they will remove all its live tissue faster than you can watch snowmelt. If you are working with a small number of trees, a garden hoe and a little perspiration will do the job adequately. Trees that are kept free of vegetation will grow twice as fast as the trees without a vegetation plan.

Another problem that I occasionally deal with is the wildlife conservation worker who gets the brush hog mower a little too close to the tree and snags the protective wire cage. After a short logic session with himself, he often concludes that because of his heavy workload, he does not have time to dismount from his tractor and straighten up the mess he made. So if you don't catch and correct this problem, your tree will be little more than fast food for the resident deer population.

If you are maintaining young pear trees, you should constantly be on the lookout for fire blight (see Pear Choices in the manual). If you don't catch and eliminate blighted branches quickly, it will usually kill young trees.

Another highly recommended action is to shake or remove all fruit from small trees before bears do it for you. You won't like how they do it—trust me on that! Deer and bear will consume the fruit even if it is not yet ripe.

Removing fruit from your young trees allows them to devote more of their energy into growth and limb development, resulting in increased size and larger fruit yields sooner.

> *If you don't remove the fruit from your young trees, the bears will be happy to do it for you!*

Periodic inspections and routine maintenance require time and effort. However, I view it as an insurance policy toward the time, money, and labor you have invested. A few years down the road, when your trees start to produce buckets of fruit and nourishment for wildlife, your efforts will be rewarded.

May all your efforts bear fruit!

PART 4

Wider Vision

Surface Mine Effects on Wildlife

(L to R) Sycamore, black cherry, and red oak growing on surface mine soil. Oak and cherry are estimated to be approximately forty-two years old, while the sycamore is less than twenty.

When huge, earth-moving machines first began turning vast expanses of forested lands upside down, it looked like the beginning of the end of a lot of quality sport-hunting real estate.

What started off looking like a modern-day tragedy actually turned into a well-disguised blessing. After the minerals were extracted, the real estate was nearly worthless to investors looking for a quick profit. Much of this land was "purchased for a song" by wildlife management agencies. It is now providing excellent hunting opportunities for sportsmen.

Initially, I questioned if these devastated locations would ever recover in a single lifetime. Soon, however, evidence began to indicate that reclaimed surface mine sites were providing increased habitat diversity that proved very beneficial to all species of wildlife. Reclaimed soil was seeded with grasses and legumes, which provides forage for deer and elk, as well as excellent brood habitat for wild turkeys. Much of this acreage was planted with tree and shrub seedlings, which provide hard and soft mast for wildlife. The end result was a forest that is more wildlife friendly and has more species (both wildlife and trees) than the original habitat.

As a sportsman, my pursuit of wildlife has evolved to the point where I do the majority of my hunting on and around reclaimed surface mines! Show me an old reclamation project surrounded with mature hardwoods, and I will put my reputation as a hunter on the line by assuring that you have found a quality hunting hotspot!

Fortunately, some things, at times, can take on greater clarity with age. I am blessed to have lived long enough to see much of this land recover to the point where it is starting to resemble its original condition. Former desolate strip mines are being recolonized by native species of trees, shrubs, and vines. Oaks, maple, black locust, sycamore, hickory, black cherry, and cucumber magnolia demonstrate the resiliency to prosper and thrive on very poor subsoils.

Unfortunately, reforestation can be a very slow, gradual process. The elimination of oxygenated-surface topsoil has been very detrimental to tree and shrub recolonization. This upper layer of soil was occupied by mycorrhizal fungi, which form a symbiotic (beneficial) relationship with tree root systems. Some experts believe approximately 98 percent of all trees and shrubs share this joint relationship.

Mycorrhizae funguses bond to a tree's root system—one species externally and another internally. The mycorrhizae assist the tree in the recruitment and absorption of water and minerals. They also defend the tree's roots from enemy funguses and parasitic root (small cylindrical worms) nematodes, while the tree's roots provide carbohydrates to the mycorrhizae.

Funguses seed themselves through spores. I expect that this is a slow process involving a lot of variables. Mycorrhizal inoculants are commercially available, and one can find a wealth of information about them on the internet—just search "mycorrhiza" for helpful information.

If one is only transplanting a limited number of seedlings, incorporation of soil or small roots from an established tree should successfully seed beneficial fungi. A problematic issue with mine spoil reclamation is that oak and hickory seedlings don't transplant well. They have very long taproots that are sheared off in the harvest process at seedling nurseries. More effort needs to be explored to determine if these species would have a higher survival rate by direct seeding at the planting site.

However, with some patience, I believe surface mines offer almost unlimited opportunities for wildlife enhancement projects. Tree and shrub species that are absent in the surrounding forest can be incorporated into a reforestation plan to provide a more consistent smorgasbord of food for wildlife. Blocks of conifer plantings are very effective in providing thermal cover for wildlife. And portions of land can be permanently maintained as herbaceous openings to provide forage for elk and deer and insects for wild turkeys.

With careful planning and well-executed habitat work, surface mine sites can exceed the wildlife carrying capacity of the original forest!

Healthy Forest Management Fundamentals

If you want to foster a healthy, stable wildlife population, you must have a diverse, healthy forest. Yes, an oak forest may provide a good food source for wildlife when the trees produce mast. Unfortunately, oak trees only fruit abundantly about every third year. In the off years, what do the critters eat?

Also, there are the disease- and insect-infestation factors to consider. Forest monocultures (one dominant tree species) are most vulnerable to diseases and insect outbreaks. The greater the species representation, the less likely these factors will become an issue and the healthier your forest will be.

Insects and diseases sweep through a forest in much the same way that a wildfire consumes trees. Imagine a large, unbroken expanse of pine or spruce. When exposed to fire, flames leapfrog from tree to tree unrestricted. If it were a diverse forest—where conifers are more widely dispersed or scattered in small clusters—the fire would likely burn itself out because of the buffer zones between the fire-vulnerable spruces.

Like fire, insects and diseases move in a similar manner by leapfrogging from target species to target species. If you don't maintain a buffer zone (other tree species) between your disease- or insect-infected trees, the consequences are sure to be total destruction. When disease or insects are found to cross buffer zones (nontarget tree species), they are exposed to predatory insects, birds, amphibians, animals, arachnoids, and fungi to prey on them, slowing or stopping their advances.

Your first composition plan should be species diversity—not creating conditions where parasitic insects can breed and multiply more rapidly than the predatory forces which control them. Yes, this may require some low-value tree species into your management plan. It is a very small price to pay for a more wildlife friendly, diverse, disease-resistant, and healthy timber stand.

If you ignore species diversity, you run the risk of watching your valuable trees being devoured by diseases or insect infestations. What was once a valuable timber stand can quickly be turned into standing firewood. The end result? The woodlot with some of these low-value species may be the one that provides the best return on equity.

Let These Stand

If your goal is managing your woodlot for wild turkeys, cucumber magnolia is a species that deserves a protective status. Black gum (tupelo) is another wildlife-friendly tree that should be added to the protected list, and American basswood (linden) likely earns a spot in the lineup too.

The fruit pod of the cucumber tree is bear candy for hungry bruins. Show me a cucumber tree with fruit on it, and I will show you evidence that bears have already been there. When the green cucumber-like seedpods ripen, they turn a brilliant red color. After a heavy freeze, the colorful pods turn a brownish black and release bright-red seeds. Seed volume can be heavy, and turkeys will gorge themselves on them.

And then there is black gum. It produces an abundance of black, pea-sized seeds that are consumed by a wide variety of wildlife. It is an important food source for wild turkeys because it retains its fruit on the branches throughout the winter. Black gum is also a tree reportedly very beneficial to honeybees.

Basswood is tremendously valuable to turkeys. It is a good honey-producing tree too! As a former beekeeper, I can verify that when the basswood is blooming, bees are heavily into honey production. It also produces a huge seed crop of pea-sized seeds that turkeys aggressively seek out.

The reason these three tree species deserve a protected status is that they are highly preferred browse for whitetail deer. With even a moderate deer population, when any of these three are eliminated, it is not likely that any stump sprout regeneration will take place, as deer will nip off any young hardwood seedlings in their infancy.

Basswood, black gum, and cucumber magnolia are all low-value timber sources. However, none in the group is ever destined to become a dominant tree species simply because of the impact deer have on them. Remember that a diverse forest is a healthy forest! Cucumber magnolia is a species I have observed growing on acidic strip main soils and appearing quite healthy and vigorous in this environment.

Sycamores self-seeding on an abandoned strip mine site

Another tree species that exhibits adaptability to reclaimed mine sites is the sycamore tree. I cannot say sycamores are highly beneficial to wildlife, but they do provide cover, are very fast growers, long-lived, and fairly valuable as a tough, durable hardwood.

Living with Invasives

"Invasive species" is a term applying to introduced varieties of bushes, shrubs, vines, and plants that have aggressive growth characteristics, capable of prospering on very poor, infertile soil types. The majority of specimens in this class are introduced (alien) from Europe or Asia. However, some native species can become very aggressive and overly dominant if landscapes are conducive to their reproduction.

The majority of alien species were introduced with the intention of improving wildlife habitat. Unfortunately, almost nobody anticipated the negative side effects that accompanied them. Regrettably, the diseases and insects that kept their numbers in check abroad were not part of the package. The end results are species aggressiveness and overpopulation.

The list of invasives is a long one—multiflora rose, autumn olive, Japanese honeysuckle, and European blackthorn are the species most often mentioned. When the topic of invasives arises, people usually divide into two groups—those who like them and those who hate them. Both factions justify some very strong arguments to support their positions.

In recent years, autumn olive has managed to surpass multiflora rose as the most problematic species in Pennsylvania. Its supporters note that at least 135 species of birds consume its fruit, and every animal in the forest from the size of a mouse to a bear voraciously consumes its berries and enclosed seeds. Autumn olive also enriches sterile, infertile soil because its root system produces prodigious amounts of nitrogen to the benefit of all encroaching grass, shrubs, and trees.

The flowers of this species are highly utilized by honeybees. At times, one can smell its nectar from hundreds of yards away. Autumn olive's twigs and new growth are browsed by deer and very high in protein. Autumn olive's abundant fruit supply also reduces wildlife's dependence on foraging agricultural crops.

This species' detractors also hold a fortified position supporting their dislike for this invasive. They are quick to point out that, as with most introduced species, their aggressiveness often surpasses and outcompetes native species, and its rank growth can eventually inhibit gradual reforestation. Autumn olive can also overtake fallow (unplowed, unmaintained) farmland, forming dense, impenetrable thickets. As with any aggressive species, once they are established, autumn olives are almost impossible to eradicate.

Conclusion

Introduced species can be beneficial to wildlife. Unfortunately, their aggressive characteristics make them almost impossible to control or eradicate. In recent years, I witnessed considerable expenditure of cash and resources to eliminate invasives at the statewide level. I believe time will demonstrate that these efforts were not a wise use of resources!

The main problem is that when a mature invasive is removed, every exposed root sprout and dormant seed will germinate. The end result—eliminate one, and many of its siblings will come to the funeral. Short of a long, expensive, intense effort, these species are here to stay!

If I were to develop a plan to control alien species' aggressiveness, I would eliminate the types of *environments* that enhance their aggressive nature. Fallow agricultural land and abandoned surface mine sites are areas of concern. Periodic mowing of agricultural land and reforestation of surface mines will curb this aggressiveness. An overhead forest canopy denies the invasives the sunlight they require to thrive.

In an effort to eliminate established autumn olive colonies, mechanically remove all mature target species in late winter. Following this subtraction, refrain from mowing, allowing the roots time to sucker, and dormant seeds time to regenerate. In late September, spray the entire targeted area with a strong herbicide such as Banvel. Very early the following spring, mow or brush the treated region to further suppress any weakened or sickened regeneration attempts by the mother plants. One may also consider a fall mowing after herbicides are allowed time to do their work. Often, damaged tissue that hasn't healed is much more susceptible to injury to freezing temperatures. (There is also less chance of getting a heavy machine stuck in often-wet spring conditions.) Immediately after mowing, quickly plant tree seedlings in an effort to establish reforestation. The newly planted seedlings should quickly establish, growing aggressively in the nitrogen-enriched (from roots of autumn olive) soil.

Yes, I do anticipate the invasives will stage a comeback attempt. However, if your seedlings have established, they will quickly overtake the invasives, eventually depriving them of the sunlight necessary for their survival. My personal selection of hardwood seedlings would include a mixture of oaks, along with chestnut, sycamore, hickory, cucumber magnolia, and black cherry—if goldenrod is not present. (Goldenrod is toxic to black cherry.) All will do well on poor, acidic soil types.

One final option for consideration is a biannual mowing of established autumn olive colonies. Yes, the established shrubs will quickly sucker sprout and mount a comeback attempt. In their efforts to resprout, they will provide a year-round, high-protein forage for deer and elk, as well as providing cover for small birds and animals.

If we can justify purchasing lime, seed, and fertilizer—and the need for multiple agricultural practices to produce a single crop of grain (which usually lasts but a period of a few short weeks)—is a biannual mowing too much to ask for a shrub base that will provide a high-protein forage and cover for wildlife all year long?

Food Plot Strategies

Interest in wildlife food plots (HBOs) in the last decade has grown in leaps and bounds and continues to grow as I write. New forage crops that benefit wildlife are being constantly introduced to satisfy the interest of savvy hunters and sportspersons.

Sometimes, the options can be overwhelming to the amateur wildlife conservationist. If you were to ask the average hunter what one should plant for deer or turkeys, they would probably respond, "Corn and buckwheat." No doubt, deer and turkeys will consume these grains enthusiastically. Unfortunately, there are a lot of negatives in planting grain crops for wildlife. For openers, annual grains consume a tremendous amount of valuable resources—time, energy, fertilizer, lime, and herbicides. Grain crops usually mature—and are consumed—at a time of year when there is an abundance of natural food sources available. However, when the snow flies and the critters are in need, the cupboards are empty.

Another fact that must be considered when working with cereal grains is that you must be willing to plant enough acreage to overwhelm the appetite of the local deer herd. This usually requires a minimum of at least five acres or more! Plant less than that, and you have done little more than provide a salad for the resident deer population.

If you have deep pockets, time, and machinery, grain crops can be utilized quite effectively. Unfortunately, the average individual or wildlife conservation organizations are subject to limitations that dictate that there be better options than resource-consuming grain crops. For decades, select grasses and legumes have proven to be the most affordable and reliable choices of food sources for wildlife, and I expect this to continue as the norm.

Before we discuss what to plant, the first order of business is to take a soil test. These can be acquired with a quick trip to your county's agricultural soil conservation service office. For about ten or fifteen dollars, you can purchase a soil-testing kit complete with instructions. You will have to complete a minimal amount of paperwork and inform the lab about what species of grass, legumes, or grains you want to plant. It usually takes a couple of weeks for the lab to process your soil sample and forward the results of the nutrient needs of your food plot to you. Don't for one minute consider planting an ounce of seed without a soil test!

Clover

In most circumstances, legumes (clover family) are more highly preferred by wildlife than grasses. However, legumes lack staying power. The usual norm is that they will persist for a period of two to three years. As deer gradually suppress their presence, grasses usually step up and occupy the legumes' absence. You can choose to add some grass seed to the legume-seed mix. But understand that the grasses will compete with your legumes. Some of the densest clover patches I ever observed had little to no grass in the stand. Almost miraculously, as clovers gradually disappear, grasses quickly fill the void.

What are the preferred varieties of clover to use? Ladino is usually the top choice, followed by (the very similar) white Dutch and alsike. South of the Mason-Dixon Line, crimson clover is reported to do well. If wild turkeys are among your targeted management species, it is wise to include bird's-foot trefoil into the seed mix. As a forage crop, trefoil is less desirable than the clovers, but it is this reduced desirability that enables it to outlast the clovers on your food plot. The most positive characteristic of trefoils is that they stimulate dense insect populations (grasshoppers, leafhoppers, etc.), and turkeys—especially poults—love insects. It is not uncommon for trefoils to persist in a stand for twenty-five years or more. Trefoil is also a member of the legume family. It is very high in protein, thrives in the poorest of soils, withstands heavy foraging by deer, and can persist for decades in plantings. All legume seedlings—such as clover—should include some trefoil.

Food Plot Grasses

Red fescue is a solid forage grass for deer—producing a seed head that is heavily utilized by turkeys—but is somewhat dominant and can, unfortunately, suppress clover and legumes.

Orchard grass is an excellent forage grass for deer. But it is of little value to turkeys and produces a coarse, rank growth that can choke out other grasses and legumes. If you include this one in your plans, go no heavier than two pounds of seed per acre.

Deer tongue is another recommended forage grass for deer, but like orchard grass, it tends to dominate and should probably be sown only in small patches. The seed heads of this plant are desirable to turkeys as well. But they should be utilized only in small, difficult locations. It is very persistent and long-lived.

Meadow foxtail is a wonderful forage grass for elk and deer. It also has a seed head that is heavily utilized by wild turkeys and is long-lived with an abundance of favorable growth characteristics and almost no negatives!

Food Plot Longevity

Managing herbaceous openings for deer may require a different strategy than creating food plots for turkeys. Plots established for deer should be fertilized adequately enough to encourage lush, nutrient-rich forage. Plots managed for turkeys should have a shorter, less dense, nonaggressive forage base. My late wildlife biologist friend, Jerry Wunz, was often quoted as saying, "If you can't see your shoes when you walk through a food plot, it is probably too thick for turkeys."

When one establishes a new seedbed on an HBO, the first three years of growth are more ideally suited to satisfy the needs of deer. The following three years of the plot's cycle is usually more conducive to the needs of turkeys due to reduced forage density. As the forage becomes thinner and less aggressive, it is much easier for turkeys—especially poults—to move around in it and catch insects and grasshoppers. Wild strawberries are apt to colonize the sparser cover. To a turkey, this is surely the equivalent of having ice cream to accompany your steak.

How much seed should you apply per acre? With fine legume seeds, the accepted norm is about six pounds per acre. Less can be used, but you will have more competition from less desirable species. Grass seeds are much larger and probably should be seeded at a heavier rate. A balanced effort would maintain separate food plots for deer and turkeys.

The life of a seedbed is usually about six years. Eventually, wildlife removing nutrients increased soil acidity, and the increased presence of invasive species such as goldenrod and aster dictates that a seedbed renewal is in order. Remember, too, all legumes in your seed mix should be inoculated. Also, if you are seeding legumes on a site that is not prone to water erosion, you will see much better results if you omit nurse species (especially annual rye grass) from the seed mix.

Cost-Saving Tip

Seed application rates can easily be reduced by half and still show satisfactory results. The problem is the difficulty of finding a process to evenly apply seed in minimal amounts. I managed to address this challenge by mixing the seed with a clean, dry, free-flowing sand and distributing the mix with a handheld, hand-cranked rotary seeder. The hand seeder also eliminates the need for a seed drill, which saves both time and money.

However, when using a hand seeder, it is absolutely necessary that your newly worked soil be seeded before the first rain falls on it. Precipitation settles and seals the soil, prohibiting the seed from planting itself on the formerly porous soil conditions.

With a broadcast seeder, you can cover an area approximately twenty-five feet wide per pass. I usually use a white string or twine to guide my footsteps as I seed. After making a pass with the seeder, I simply move the string to guide me on the next pass. If you have seed remaining, you can lightly make passes with your seed applicator perpendicular to your original application direction to further ensure complete coverage.

Frost seeding has also proven to be an effective method of applying seed. The biggest problem with frost seeding is that you may find yourself waiting for freezing conditions that never materialize. In most instances, frost seeding is only effective immediately after snowmelt or just prior to the first of the season snowfall. Once again, frost seeding can eliminate the need for a grain drill and tractor.

With limited finances, I once seeded a food plot immediately after the dozer work was completed. Despite the very rough soil conditions, the rain, weather, and elements leveled the rough ground much better than I had anticipated—just another example of stretching resources!

May all your efforts bear fruit!

Parting Shots

Dos and Don'ts

1. Do not plant trees or shrubs near the root zones of black walnut trees. Walnuts produce allelopaths (toxins) that will kill your trees.

2. Avoid using snow fence or similar products to fence your trees. They provide mice and voles overhead protection and encourage their presence. You want hawks and owls to have an unobstructed view of the terrain.

3. Don't use spiral trunk protectors. They are nearly worthless.

4. Always keep your protective wire cages around your trees one foot off the ground. Ignore this advice, and it will cost you your tree. If the top of the cage is not five feet above the ground, the deer will forage on the top of your trees and kill them.

5. Give your trees an occasional application of fertilizer. The advantages are many.

6. If you are using field fence (best value) to protect young trees, make certain that the tighter mesh of the wire is at the *top* of your protection cage. If you do not, the deer will reach through the wire and eat your tree into submission.

7. Never expose the roots of young trees or seedlings to freezing temperatures. Prune your trees properly when they are young. A tree with a good limb structure requires little long-term maintenance.

8. When working with unskilled labor, make certain to check their work constantly.

9. Always try to match tree and shrub species to soil conditions—soil, dryness, alkaline, acetic, etc.

10. Do not prune your trees if subzero temperatures are still a threat.

11. Remove fruit from small trees in their early developmental stages. Trees will put more energy into growing faster and larger. The end result will be that your trees will produce more abundant yields more quickly, and you will greatly reduce conflicts with bears.

12. Never plant wild cherry where goldenrod is established. Toxins from the goldenrod will kill black cherry.

Food for Thought

In the opening pages of this manual, I expressed my concerns over the environmental impact that an out-of-balance deer herd can inflict on a forest. I want to leave you with a few stories of friends who had some lessons in this "school of hard luck." Hopefully, their experiences will give you, the reader, a new respect for the need to clearly manage deer populations.

Evidence of deer overpopulation: obvious browse line on hemlock trees and a clear, clean tree understory

Sheldon's Story

My friend Sheldon was concerned about the lack of cover on his hunting club's property. He sought my advice on what would be the best species of conifer to plant for cover. I recommended his club members plant white spruce because it is very resistant to browse impact from deer. However, Sheldon's friends were strongly leaning toward planting white *pine*.

I expressed my concern that this was a species on which deer commonly feed. My friend's response was "Joe, with all the doe allocations in recent years, we really have the deer knocked back, and we don't have many deer left."

Somewhat skeptical of what Sheldon's idea of what "low deer numbers" represented, I nevertheless agreed that if whitetail numbers really were low, white pine seedlings might survive. The club members chose to plant white pines. Sheldon regularly reported to me throughout the year that the pine planting was faring well. I was cautiously optimistic that with a little luck, the deer population would find food without touching the young seedlings. Unfortunately, when one relies on luck, the only type you usually receive is bad luck.

Sheldon confirmed this when he reported to me in early March, "Joe, there is not one pine seedling left. The deer found every last one of them!"

Hunting club members eventually grew weary of fighting with deer and installed an electric fence around their habitat plantings. It's amazing how deer can change our perspective on what suitable population levels are. Were deer numbers around Sheldon's camp as low as he claimed them to be? It's quite possible that his estimates may have been spot on.

A heavily forested region near my home had a burgeoning deer population for an extended period of time. The old saying that "all good things must come to an end" proved to be factual. After deer numbers plummeted to very low levels, the department of wildlife conducted a thermal imaging study to determine accurate deer densities. It was discovered that the area which formerly held fifty to sixty deer per square mile now had only 3.6 whitetails per square mile.

How do you correct a wildlife management mess like this? There are no easy solutions. You cannot force hunters to hunt where deer numbers are so pathetically low. And trying to convince them that they must harvest more animals in order for the habitat to recover is nearly impossible! Completely eliminating the harvest of female deer in this forest would not make deer numbers increase because the habitat is suppressed by the few remaining deer to the point where it cannot recover.

The only alternative is massive deer exclosures. But such extreme measures voraciously consume wildlife resources. An even better solution to avoiding wildlife management issues is to listen and act on the recommendations of wildlife biologists and foresters. These professionals are highly trained to make decisions based on facts and meticulous observations, not on emotions and unrealistic desires.

Gary's Story

Hawthorn narrowly escaping being "browsed to death"

Gary was another coworker who came to me asking advice. He was concerned that despite his hunting camp and the surrounding camps having a policy of not harvesting does, the deer population was on a steady decline. I managed to convince my worried friend that the problem was most likely attributed to habitat depletion from high deer numbers. Gary and his brother decided to take action and do some wildlife habitat enhancement work. The siblings arose early one Saturday morning and secured several dozen raspberry seedlings from their mom's raspberry patch and headed to camp.

The brothers spent the rest of the morning planting and watering the brambles before returning to camp for a little R&R and a quick lunch. After lunch, the guys decided to check their plantings for signs of wilt or transplant shock. Indeed, they were shocked! They discovered that while they were foraging at the camp dinner table, the deer were foraging on the newly transplanted raspberry seedlings! The hungry grazers found and consumed every new transplant!

Question—if raspberry seedlings could not survive a couple of hours, what chance does an oak, hickory, or young grapevine seedling have of surviving the six or eight *years* required to grow beyond the reach of foraging deer? Hopefully, you are starting to get the picture!

Another Sheldon Story

I offered my friend Sheldon eight two-year-old mountain ash seedlings, which he graciously accepted. I cautioned him that when planted, the young seedlings would need protective fencing immediately because this was a species highly prized as a food source by deer. Sheldon planted the seedlings that evening and planned to return the following day to fence them.

You guessed it—when he returned the next day, fencing in tow, he discovered that the deer already found them. When you have done habitat improvement work as long as I have, it is very easy to predict the actions of deer.

Decision Time

I had just completed my last wildlife habitat improvement presentation of the day at a Jakes' youth event when three middle-aged gentlemen approached me.

"Hey, buddy, can we have a few moments of your time?" one of the men called out.

"Most certainly. What's on your mind?" I asked.

The men began to tell me that they attended my presentation the previous year and were paying attention to the manner in which I talked to the kids. They listened to the way I explained the need to pay attention to stump sprouts in new timber cuttings to determine if the deer herd is in balance with the habitat.

"So my friends and I started to study stump sprouts too, and there's nothing left! The SOB are eating everything!" they growled.

I answered with a question, "Pretty scary, isn't it?"

"Really scary," they all echoed.

We exchanged small talk as I expressed my concern about the lack of education that is so prevalent among our nation's deer hunters, as the group nodded their heads in agreement. I complimented my new friends for having open minds and further expressed my gratitude for their efforts to be observant. I urged them to share their observations with both their hunting and nonhunting friends. They assured me that they would do just that. We chatted briefly, and they shook my hand and expressed their appreciation for my efforts in working with our young people.

As I mentioned in this manual, I have spent much of my adult life enhancing wildlife habitat. Having my efforts constantly exposed to the foraging activity of deer has been an incredible educational experience for me. It has given me a clear understanding of the impact that deer have on our forest and the need to control their numbers.

I have also worked and interacted with many dedicated professionals in the wildlife management field and am extremely confident that these people know what they are doing. And no, they don't hate deer! They love all wildlife, dedicating their lives to the protection and management of these resources. As sportsmen and hunters, it is time to give these professionals our trust and confidence, letting them know we have their backs. They have earned and deserve our support! United we stand, divided we fall. The choice is ours.

Special Thanks

I owe many thanks to my son James for working with me while writing this manual. Jim was a very good student in school, and his literary skills were very helpful to me. It is possible that some of my son's bad days in school may have been better than Dad's good days in my educational process. Jim never hesitated to take time from his busy schedule to edit my writings or offer suggestions. Lesson learned—if you don't do well in school, make certain that your sons and daughters do. If you treat them well, they will help you when in need!

Our graphic designer friend Eric Beeler took some of my hand-drawn illustrations and added a professional's touch, breaking out his pen and ink to bring the sketches up to the level worthy of a published work. I was particularly pleased with the "whip graft" illustration featured in both the table of contents and "Converting Wild Apple and Wild Pear Trees into More Productive and Disease-Resistant Cultivars" section of the book.

I also owe my longtime outdoor writer friend, Shirley Grenoble, much appreciation and a big thank-you for converting my cursive writing into typed print and offering me some worthwhile suggestions to enhance my efforts. Having suffered a traumatic brain injury that robbed one of my hands the majority of its motor skills—and missing a digit on my other hand—it is quite obvious that I could not have completed this manual without help. Lesson learned—if you keep yourself surrounded by good people, they will have your back!

It was also under Shirley's leadership as president of the Pennsylvania chapter of the NWTF that she recognized my love of wildlife enhancement work and appointed me as the first chairman of our superfund habitat review committee. I like to think that Shirley recognized commitment. She made that decision several decades ago, and my dedication to wildlife habitat enhancement work continues to endure. Once again, Shirley, thank you for all the help, but most of all, thank you for your friendship!

Reflections

What makes a man spend almost four decades of his life growing, planting, and caring for trees that provide food and cover for wildlife? What motivated the same guy to plant enough trees and seedlings that the four-inch-wide blade on his tree-planting bar—which started out square—is now worn nearly as round as a marble?

My answer—I like the results, and I know these efforts are making a difference.

What motivated me to take such a deep interest in doing wildlife enhancement work? It all began in my late teens when I was lying down boot leather in the woods, looking for wild turkeys and whitetail deer. My travels led me to an old, abandoned strip mine on which somebody completed some serious wildlife habitat improvement work. There were rows of evenly spaced black locust trees with their nitrogen-establishing roots, supporting a lush stand of tender, green grass. Well-worn trails gave witness that there was a robust deer population.

Bittersweet is providing an abundance of fruit and cover for wildlife. This productive vine will hold fruit throughout the winter months.

Crab apple trees were numerous. Fruit on the other trees ranged from pea- to quarter-sized and colored various shades of red, orange, and yellow. Rose bushes held an abundance of ruby-like rose hips. And there were brilliant orange bittersweet berries as well. Further complementing the wildlife smorgasbord were bush-like shrubs hanging heavy with loads of dull-colored red berries with pepper-like tan speckles.

The place was alive with wildlife. There were plenty of turkey tracks in the mud around water puddles. Small piles of seed hulls with the kernels neatly removed were evident at the bases of the crab apple trees—perhaps the work of mice, voles, or chipmunks. Flocks of cedar waxwings and robins were busy plundering the berry bushes and crab apple trees.

Predators also took notice of this abundance of protein. Fox scat was plentiful on the tram roads. Being observant, I often saw a red-tailed hawk circling overhead or perched on a distant snag, perhaps watching for a robin, mouse, or chipmunk preoccupied with stuffing itself on the abundant food.

Almost like some grand experiment, a large portion of the surface mine had no wildlife enhancement efforts present. It was largely abandoned in the hope of healing itself. Here one could find an occasional clump of aspen or a few widely scattered black birches surrounded by plenty of exposed, rocky subsoil. A mouse would have had a tough time scratching out a living here!

I also purchased my first laminated fiberglass hunting bow during this period. I learned quickly the best place to ambush a buck was near the many fruit trees of abandoned homesteads that dotted the Allegheny Plateau of western Pennsylvania.

Unfortunately, the majority of these remaining trees are nearing or have surpassed the century mark in age. They are fast falling victim to Father Time and are dying off at an alarming rate. I have within me a strong desire to see that these trees are replaced because I want future generations to experience the pleasure of observing wildlife and hunting near these magnificent food sources.

How much longer will I continue to do this work? Probably as long as I am able. Do I like planting trees? Heck no! It's a lot of hard work.

What I do love is the results I see. May all your efforts bear fruit!

About the Author

Joe Krug has dedicated nearly four decades of his life to better understand and improve the quality of wildlife habitat. Joe served on the board of directors of the Pennsylvania chapter of the National Wild Turkey Federation (NWTF). He holds life memberships in the NWTF, NRA, the Rocky Mountain Elk Foundation, and the National Trappers Association. He received local, regional, state, and national recognition for his wildlife conservation efforts and is the recipient of the following awards:

- Dr. Roger M. Latham Award
    Given to the Pennsylvania State Chapter of the National Wild Turkey Federation board of director who exhibits leadership and responsibility above and beyond their duties
- James E. Wilhelm Conservation Award
    For inspiring and instructing proper wildlife improvement efforts and creating new habitat
- Dr. David D. Wanless Award
    Honors an NWTF member of the Pennsylvania State Chapter who makes outstanding contributions to further the goals and purpose of the Pennsylvania State Chapter.
- Local Chapter President's Award
    Given for having served numerous terms as president of the Allegheny Mountain Chapter of the NWTF

- Induction into the Pennsylvania Turkey Hunters Hall of Fame

    For commitment to the resource and passion for turkey hunting
- Blair County Conservation Officers Association Award

    For contributions to wildlife and all Pennsylvania sportsmen and habitat improvement work on State Game Lands of Pennsylvania.
- Soisson Recreation Award

    For efforts to improve wildlife habitat and sport-hunting opportunities in Cambria County, Pennsylvania
- Department of Conservation and Natural Resources Award

    For efforts to improve wildlife habitat in Gallitzin State Forest
- Roger M. Latham Sportsmen Service Award

    National award given to the top wildlife conservationist who is not employed as a professional wildlife manager
- Pennsylvania Working Together for Wildlife Conservation Award

    Twice recognized by the Pennsylvania Game Commission for wildlife habitat improvement work efforts on Pennsylvania State Game Lands
- Pennsylvania Loyal Order of the Silver Spurs Award

    For having served ten years as an elected official of the Pennsylvania Chapter of the NWTF and recognition for having previously received the majority of the chapter's most prestigious awards

The author is an avid deer and turkey hunter. He also has been on numerous elk hunts, several adventures for moose, and one excursion for African plains game. On some of these excursions, he deserved better luck and on others, better luck than he deserved! He has life memberships in the National Rifle Association, Rocky Mountain Elk Foundation, and the National Wild Turkey Federation while maintaining annual memberships in Ducks Unlimited, the National Trappers Association, and Keystone Elk Country Alliance.

He is a firm believer that all sportsmen should strongly commit to give back to the resource. It is this belief that has led him on a nearly four-decade commitment to improve wildlife habitat. He was fortunate to befriend by an outstanding wildlife biologist and many wildlife conservation management professionals. Through their help and guidance, he has made many lifelong friendships.

The author received the bulk of his education in wildlife management from "the school of hard knocks." When things did not go as planned, he simply backtracked, figured out what went wrong, and developed a plan to fix it. His nearly four decades of experience in wildlife conservation work will keep you from acquiring your education at that same rigorous institution.